ATHLETIC
SCHOLARSHIPS

ATHLETIC
SCHOLARSHIPS

DAVID LAHEY
MAKING YOUR SPORTS PAY

Warwick Publishing Inc.
Toronto   Los Angeles

Athletic Scholarships

Published by the Warwick Publishing Group
Warwick Publishing Inc., 24 Mercer Street, Toronto, Ontario M5V 1H3
Warwick Publishing Inc., 1300 Alexandria, Los Angeles, California 90027

Cover Design: Dave Hader
Text Design: JAQ

ISBN 1-895629-06-3

Distributed in the United States and Canada by:
Firefly Books Ltd.
250 Sparks Avenue
Willowdale, ON.
M2H 2S4

Printed and bound in Canada.

Contents

Preface

Chapter 1 Terminology 1

Chapter 2 In What Level Do I Belong? 5

Chapter 3 Recruiting – Am I a Blue Chipper? 21

Chapter 4 Selecting a College 25

Chapter 5 The Academics –
A Campus By Campus Analysis 103

Summary 155

Life After College 157

Appendices 158

Selected Bibliography 175

Sample Application Forms 176

To

Kelly-Anne, Curtis and Jennifer Lahey,
athletes of tomorrow

Patricia Stamler-Lahey

in Memory of
Syd Howe and Francis Howe,
two people who wanted the best for their grandchildren

and to a true teacher
who helped direct my career path,
my dad,
Orv Lahey.

Preface

Scholarships today are the target of most intelligent student athletes. Scholarships, grants and loans through financial assistance have provided thousands of young athletes from — not only North America — but around the world with access to a positive future and a prosperous career upon graduation. Each institution in this book offers opportunities to earn a college/university education in exchange for the enrichments a student athlete brings to the particular campus.

A college experience which contains the participation in a collegiate sport has been the highlight of thousands of athletes' lives. The learning atmosphere that a person at the college level experiences helps develop an individual in a manner that sets them head and shoulders above the crowd. A great many student athletes have used college sports as their vehicle to careers in business, the medical field, law, and technology. Many talented collegians who excel in their sports have received professional contracts after they graduate or choose to finish their college eligibility. We also see each year college athletes participate in international competition for their country.

CHAPTER 1

Terminology

IN CANADA, THERE are community colleges and universities. Both of these mean higher education but only universities have the power to grant degrees. In the U.S. the system is different. A prospective student should be cautious and look closely at the actual degrees offered by these institutions. In other words, let the buyer beware. There are American Community colleges which offer two year diplomas — not degrees. You may also find American colleges which offer two year associate degrees. Next, there are four year colleges and universities. The colleges award diplomas for an undergraduate's bachelor's degree. The universities can grant bachelor's degrees but they also give masters and doctorate degrees. This is not to say either one is better. Most American parents will send their children to college and save their entire life to do so!

When you enter college the first year you are called a "freshman." The second year you are a "sophomore", the third a "junior" and finally a "senior."

Most college athletic programs will have three levels of athletics: the varsity or college team, junior varsity, and club. The varsity is where the action is. This is the number one team. Junior varsity, in many programs, will be used as a feeder to help develop an incoming freshman. Your goal must be to aim for varsity. The club level usually, but not always, provides no financial assistance. This level is non-competitive, low skill athletics. Many schools begin their programs by introducing the sport to their campus at the club level. This method allows them to test the college community for support.

Traditionally, the better colleges, academically, have been situated in the eastern United States. For hundreds of years, the northeastern section of the U.S. has developed schools such as Harvard, Yale, Princeton, and Brown, which are part of the Ivy League set. These Ivy League schools are extremely well known for academic excellence. Many graduates from these go on to post graduate careers in law, medicine and business. The increasing need for well educated people in the northeast also led to the unique development of smaller Ivy League style campuses who have formed an athletic association called NESCAC or New England Small College Athletic Conference. Here students must also perform extremely well on their entrance board scores or "SAT's." These schools include: Hamilton, Williams, Bowdoin, Middlebury and Colby. They offer smaller (less than 1,900 students) campuses and Ivy League calibre professors. Graduates also go on to careers in law, medicine, upper level managerial positions and banking. Like the Ivy League schools these smaller colleges are quite expensive for a four year education. As of February 1993, the average cost for tuition, room and board and books at these private schools is over $20,000 U.S. per year. Fortunately though, because of the large endowments in these prestigious schools, there is a large pool of monies available for financial assistance. Notice I use the word "assistance", not "scholarship." In smaller schools and the Ivy League, scholarships strictly on the basis of athletic skills are not allowed. All monies allocated to incoming freshmen are done on the basis of financial need. In the Appendix, you will find two application samples for financial aid from Middlebury College in Vermont and Harvard University. By examining them you can get a feel for the kinds of questions you will be required to answer.

At most colleges in the U.S., the cost will appear more expensive than in Canada for an education. Canadians must keep in mind that Canadian schools are heavily subsidized by the government. The actual cost of a year at the highly rated Queen's University, Kingston, Ontario, for an average student in 1992 is:

Tuition (Commerce) & student interest fees	$ 1,900.00
Room & Board	$ 4,600.00
Books	$ 1,300.00
Transportation	$ 700.00
Misc./Personal (8 months)	$ 1,200.00
TOTAL	**$ 9,700.00**

With this figure as a comparison, many U.S. schools will, at first, look very expensive. However, do not be shocked to see a $20,000+ price tag on a private college like Harvard, Yale or Stanford. You will be glad to know that over 30% of all students at such campuses receive some form of financial assistance just based on their family resources. Scholarship assistance is readily available to promising incoming student athletes. These funds are only made available after the student has been accepted academically by the college. For example, when I attended Hamilton College, N.Y., as a freshman, my actual cost was far less than it would have been at five-star-rated Queen's University. I also received an excellent campus job coaching ladies' ice hockey and a small percentage long term loan.

In my experience, once you have performed well academically and have made the varsity team, increasingly more monies become available with each coming year. Other factors, such as the number of family members attending college, your parents' net income after tax and the value of their home on paper, will affect your financial package. The key term here is negotiation. Let the financial office know of your true need for scholarship monies. You must convince the financial officer that your academic/athletic skills are a much needed item by the college.

Aside from the most expensive private colleges, there are numerous less expensive state schools. Many of these offer excellent academic/athletic environments. These schools are larger, government run and subsidized campuses with similar costs to universities in Canada. Schools such as Michigan State University and Notre Dame University are big name campuses which provide full scholarships based, not on financial need, but rather on athletic ability. Financial aid is, of course, also available at these institutions.

Only Division I and II schools can offer a scholarship based solely on athletic ability. The number of scholarships available varies from sport to sport. Division III schools can attract student athletes with financial aid packages based on the perceived need for financial assistance.

CHAPTER 2

In What Level Do I Belong?

Many young athletes dream of playing for the best college team in the nation. Unfortunately, the reality is that there are only so many spots open on the athletic squads each year with hundreds of qualified candidates seeking to fill them. The tendency is to over-estimate our skills and abilities. For example, when I was an incoming freshman, there was a young man who "hyped" himself by telling of his credentials at every passing moment such that we all thought he must be the next Wayne Gretzky. Well, when we hit the ice this "New Jersey Rocket" was more like a small firecracker. He never made the team and I feel he had selected the wrong college. This same story was related to me by football, basketball and baseball college coaches.

It is difficult to know what level a player should aspire to prior to his college selection. There are so many choices. Someone with a good high school education could attend many state colleges all across the U.S. as well as many universities in Canada. It really depends on your academic background (GPA), SAT score and campus size preference.

There are hundreds of Division I schools, Division II schools and Division III schools. Academically, many Division III are far superior to Division II and Division I. Athletically Division I has the best levels (generally) in which to compete.

With all these programs it is hard to know the level of athletics to which an individual belongs. The first step, according to many head coaches, is to talk to a guidance counsellor. Meet with a high school counsellor and speak with him/her about your academic record, relating your plans to combine academics with college athletics. The counsellor can obtain for you information on various entrance requirements, the size of the campus(s) and the kinds of tests you will need to complete. Keep in mind that most U.S. colleges require all students to complete the SAT's (standard aptitude tests). In some cases a test is required to determine your proficiency in English if your mother tongue is other than English. These tests are held in each city across the United States. These tests are held three times a year in major Canadian centers and throughout Europe by contacting a major university. Contact your guidance department for details.

The second step in deciding your athletic level is simply ask your high school/junior coach for an unbiased view of your game. Tell him what your objective is. Does he think you have the determination to combine school with the competitive life of college athletics and still graduate with a degree? In what level does he/she think you should compete?

The third step is to visit a few campuses and watch some games. Sit in the stands and try to picture yourself playing with that particular college team. This is the real eye opener. You will get a very good picture of the differences of the various levels of skill and speed by simply watching games between Division II schools and between Division III schools.

Most U.S. colleges, offering athletics will have scouts ("bird dogs") who visit hundreds of schools, fields and arenas across U.S., Canada and now Europe looking for prospective candidates. They attend many high school, junior college and summer games and speak with coaches and parents to learn about players. These scouts attempt to learn the players strengths which could affect his life as a student athlete. All colleges I examine in this book are members of the largest and strongest athletic association — the NCAA. There are several other athletic associations available but the mix of academics and athletics takes a back seat to the NCAA. The NCAA is governed by strict regulations which limit paid campus visits, contact with actual college personnel and so on. Some of these regulations are reprinted in part on the following pages which are taken from the 1991-92 NCAA Guide for the College-Bound Student-Athlete, (Overland, Kansas, (913)339-1906).

Canadian Universities are now becoming very good development schools for many collegiate sports. There are now some direct links to the professional levels in hockey and football. Financial aid assistance through provincial government grants and loans are available. No SAT scores are needed but competition can be keen.

Schools vary in Canada from several top notch 5 star rated universities like Queen's University down to 4 star McGill University and 1 star University of Quebec at Trois Riviere.

NCAA Incoming Student/Athlete Restrictions

It is very important to realize that the NCAA has strict regulations for incoming and participating college student athletes. Some of their regulations are reprinted courtesy of the NCAA office.

There have been numerous academic requirements placed on incoming college freshmen. This is a much needed improvement.

Academic Eligibility

If you want to practice and play your freshman year at an NCAA Division I college you must satisfy the requirements of NCAA Bylaw 14.3, commonly known as Proposition 48. This means you must:

1. Graduate from high school;
2. Attain a grade-point average of 2,000 (based on a maximum of 4,000) in a successfully completed core curriculum of at least 11 academic courses. This core curriculum includes at least three years in English, two in mathematics, two in social science and two in natural or physical science — including at least one laboratory class, if offered by the high school.
3. Achieve a 700 combined score on the SAT verbal and math sections or an 18 composite score on the ACT.
4. Several core courses are now required. These are three units of English (each unit requires approximately 180 classroom instructional hours). Two units of mathematics including instruction in algebra, geometry, trigonometry, statistics or calculus.

Two units are also required in social sciences such as economics, psychology, government or sociology. Two units in the natural or physical science area like biology, chemistry, physics or environmental science are now required. The last core area includes 2 more of the core areas above or foreign language computer science or philosophy areas. There are strict core-curriculum interpretation followed very closely especially for Division I entrance. See the NCAA guide for the College-Bound Student Athlete. Division II colleges require the same initial academic eligibility standards as Division I. Your SAT or ACT must be taken on a national testing date. You may not use residual or regional tests to meet Bylaw 14.3.

Ask your high school guidance counsellor for the NCAA Guide to the College Freshman Eligibility Require-ments for NCAA Divisions I and II Institutions. The guide contains a detailed description of the bylaw.

If you have a learning disability or are physically handicapped, contact the NCAA office for additional information

Courtesy: Hamilton College, Clinton, N.Y.

about the application of Bylaw 14.3. Bylaw 14.3 requirements do not apply to Division III. There are special condi-
tions taken into consideration allowing for a waiver of Bylaw
14.3 requirements.

Financial Aid

Student athletes at Division I or II colleges may receive
tuition and fees, room and board and books for each acad-
mic year. You are eligible for this aid as a freshman if you
meet Bylaw 14.3 or have graduated from high school with an
overall gradepoint average of 2,000.

There is no guaranteed four year scholarship. An athletics scholarship is awarded for no more than one academic
year. It may be renewed each year for a maximum of five
years within a six year period. This pertains to both Divisions
I and II.

In some cases, you may receive additional financial assistance from certain governmental programs, such as the G.I.
Bill of Rights or the Pell Grants. Ask your college's financial
aid office for more information about these programs.

If you receive a scholarship from your high school or
local civic or booster club, tell your college's recruiter so he
or she can notify the school's financial aid office. This will
probably reduce the college scholarship package offered.

A student athlete's aid at a Division III college is based
on financial need and may not be associated with athletic
ability. Parents' income, net worth, cash flow situations play
a big role in financial aid to Division III student athletes.

Recruiting (Division I)

As a prospective student athlete you must be careful to realize you will become a "prospective student athlete" if a college coach:

1. Provides you with transportation to the college campus
2. Entertains you in any way (meals, tickets, movies, rides, etc.) on campus, except you may receive a complimentary admission to an athletics event on campus when you visit with a group tour, such as the high school band.
3. Calls you or any member of your family, or
4. Visits you or any member or your family anywhere other than the college campus.

No alumni or representatives of a college's athletics interest (boosters or reps) can be involved in your recruiting. There can be no phone calls or letters from boosters.

The booster restriction does not apply to a college's regular admissions program for all prospective students, including non-athletes.

You (or your family) may not receive any benefit, inducement or arrangement such as cash, clothing, cars, improper expenses, transportation, gifts or loans to encourage you to sign a National Letter of Intent or to attend an NCAA school. You are not to receive letters from coaches or faculty members until September 1 at the beginning of your junior year in high school.

A college coach may contact you in person only after you have completed your junior year of high school. Phone calls and letters from faculty members, students and coaches (but not boosters) are permitted at any time after this point.

Any face-to-face meeting between a college coach and you or your parents, during which any of you say more than "hello" is a contact. Furthermore, any face-to-face meeting that is prearranged, or occurs at your high school or at any competition or practice site is a contact, regardless of the conversation. These contacts are not permissible "bumps". If you meet a coach and say more than "hello", that is a contact.

In sports, except football, basketball and ice hockey, contacts are limited to two away from your high school and two (with the permission of your high school principal) at your high school.

In football, a coach may contact you three times away from your high school and once per week (with the permission of your high school principal) at your high school during December 1 through Saturday after the first day for signing of the National Letter of Intent.

In basketball, a coach may contact you three times away from your high school and once per week (with the permission of your high school principal) at your high school (maximum of three such contacts in women's basketball) during September 17 through October 7 and March 1 through the Saturday after the first day for the spring signing of the National Letter of Intent.

In ice hockey, a coach may contact you three times away from your high school and three times (with the permission of your high school principal) at your high school.

A coach may attend your practices and games to evaluate your athletic ability at any time, except in the sports of football and basketball, which have specified contact and evaluation periods. So, if you are a football or basketball recruit, learn the contact and evaluation periods.

You can visit any campus any time at your own expense. On such a visit, you may receive complimentary admissions to a game on that campus and a tour of off-campus practice and competition sites within 30 miles of the campus.

As a senior in high school, you may receive only one expense-paid (official) visit to a particular campus. This restriction applies even if you are being recruited in more than one sport.

During your official visit (which may not exceed 48 hours), you may receive round-trip transportation between your home (or high school) and the campus. You (and your parents and spouse) may receive food and lodging from the college. In addition, you and your family may be entertained (for example, movies, campus activities, visits to local interest sites) by athletics staff members, provided the entertainment is within 30 miles of the campus and is not excessive. A student host may help you become acquainted with campus life. The host may be paid $20 per day to cover expenses; however, the money cannot be used to purchase college souvenirs.

Your official visit is one of the most important aspects of the recruiting process. Use it to learn as much as possible about the college. Talk to as many coaches, faculty members and students as possible during your visit.

Remember, the college you choose will be your home for the next four years. Although you can always apply to transfer schools it is a headache, so choose carefully.

Recruiting (Division II)

You become a "prospective student athlete" if a college coach:

1. Provides you with transportation to the college campus
2. Entertains you in any way (meals, tickets, movies, rides, etc.) on campus, except you may receive a complimentary admission to an athletics event on campus when you visit with a group tour, such as the high schools band
3. Calls you or any member of your family, or
4. Visits you or any member of your family anywhere other than the college campus.

NO alumni or representatives of a college's athletics interest (boosters or reps) can be involved in your recruiting; however, you may receive telephone calls and letters from boosters, faculty members, students and coaches.

You (or your family) may not receive any benefit, inducement or arrangement such as cash, clothing, cars, improper expenses, transportation, gifts or loans to encourage you to sign a National Letter of Intent or to attend an NCAA school.

A college coach may contact you in person only after you have completed your junior year of high school.

Any face-to-face meeting between a college coach and you or your parents, during which any of you say more than "hello" is a contact. Furthermore, any face-to-face meeting that is prearranged, or occurs at your high school or at any competition or practice site is a contact, regardless of the conversation. These contacts are not permissible "bumps." If you meet a coach and say more than "hello", that is a contact.

In sports except football, basketball and ice hockey, contacts are limited to two away from your high schools and two (with the permission of your high school principal) at your high school.

In football, a coach may contact you three times away from your high school and three times (with the permission of your high school principal) at your high school during December 1 through Saturday after the first day for signing of the National Letter of Intent.

In basketball, a coach may contact you three times away from your high school and three times (with the permission of your high school principal) at your high school (maximum of three such contacts in women's basketball) during September 7 through October 14 and March 1 through the Saturday after the first day for the spring signing of the National Letter of Intent.

A coach may attend your practices and games to evaluate your athletic ability at any time, except in the sports of football and basketball, which have specified contact and evaluation periods. So, again, if you are a football or basketball recruit, learn the contact and evaluation periods.

With the permission of your high schools' director of athletics, you may try out for a college team before enrollment. The tryout must occur after you have completed your high school eligibility and may include test to evaluate your strength, speed, agility and sports skills. Except in the sports of football, ice hockey, lacrosse, soccer and wrestling, the tryout may include competition.

You can visit any campus any time at your own expense. On such a visit, you may receive complimentary admissions to a game on that campus, a tour of off-campus practice and competition sites within 30 miles of the campus and a meal in the college's on-campus student dining facilities.

During your senior year in high school, you may receive only one expense-paid (official) visit to a particular campus and you may receive no more than five such visits. This restriction applies even if you are being recruited in more than one sport.

During your official visit (which may not exceed 48 hours), you may receive round-trip transportation between your home (or high school) and the campus.

During your official visit, you (and your parents and spouse) may receive food and lodging from the college. In addition, you and your family may be entertained (for example, movies, campus activities, visits to local interest sites) by athletics staff members, provided the entertainment is within 30 miles of the campus and is not excessive.

During your official visit, a student host may help you become acquainted with campus life. The host may be given $10 per day to cover expenses; however, the money cannot be used to purchase college souvenirs.

As previously stated, your official visit is one of the most important aspects of the recruiting process. Use it to learn as much as possible about the college. Talk to as many coaches, faculty members and students as possible during your visit.

Remember, the college you choose will be your home for the next four years. Be selective and shop carefully. Make certain to review the NCAA Student Guide.

Recruiting (Division III)

Even though no direct athletic scholarships are permitted you become a "prospective student athlete" if a college coach:

1. Provides you with transportation to the college campus
2. Entertains you in any way (meals, tickets, movies, rides, etc.) on campus, except you may receive a complimentary admission to an athletics even on campus when you visit with a group tour, such as the high school band
3. Calls you or any member of your family, or
4. Visits you or any member of your family anywhere other than the college campus.

You (or your family) may not receive any benefit, inducement or arrangement such as cash, clothing, cars, improper expenses, transportation, gifts or loans to encourage you to sign a National Letter of Intent or to attend any NCAA college.

An athletics department staff member, alumni or representative of a college's athletics interest (boosters or reps) may contact you in person only after you have completed your junior year of high school; however, there is no limit on the number of contacts.

You can visit any campus any time at your own expense. On such a visit, you may receive complimentary admissions to a game on that campus, a tour of off-campus practice and competition sites within 30 miles of the campus, a meal in the college's on-campus student dining facilities, and housekeeping, provided it is available to all visiting students.

During your senior year in high school, you can make only one expense-paid (official) visit to a particular campus; however, there is no limit on the number of campuses that you may visit if you initially enroll in a Division III College.

During your official visit (which may not exceed 48 hours), you may receive round-trip transportation between your home (or high school) and the campus.

During your official visit, you (and your parents and spouse) may receive food and lodging from the college. In addition, you and your family may be entertained (for example movies, campus activities, visits to local interest sites) by athletics staff members, provided the entertainment is within 30 miles of the campus and is not excessive.

During your official visit, a student host may help you become acquainted with campus life. The host may be given $20 per day to cover expenses; however, the money cannot be used to purchase college souvenirs.

Again, your official visit is one of the most important aspects of the recruiting process. Use it to learn as much as possible about the college. Talk to as many coaches, faculty members and students as possible during your visit.

Remember, the college you choose will be your home for the next four years. Choose wisely.

Reprinted Courtesy of NCAA, "Guide to College Bound Student Athlete", Mission, Kansas. November 1991.

National Letter of Intent

The National Letter of Intent is administered by the Collegiate Commissioners Association, not the NCAA. If you have questions about the National Letter of Intent, contact the conference office of the college you are interested in attending.

Remember, do not sign any institutional or conference letter of intent (or financial aid agreement) before the National Letter of Intent signing date. Always check the signing date with the NCAA as it pertains to your sport. The telephone numbers for the various conferences will be of help to you below.

Division I Conferences

American South	504-834-6600
Assn. of Mid-Continent University	414-494-4494

Atlantic Coast	919-282-8800
Atlantic 10	201-933-5450
Big East	401-272-9108
Big Eight	816-471-5088
Big Sky	208-345-5393
Big South	803-248-9693
Big Ten	312-885-3933
Colonial	804-285-1384
East Coast	215-222-2700
Eastern College (ECAC)	617-771-5060
ECAC Metro	201-939-5909
Gateway	314-645-8760
High Country	307-766-3282
Ivy Group	609-452-6426
Metro Atlantic	203-368-6969
Metro	404-395-6444
Mid-American	419-249-7177
Mid-Eastern	919-275-9961
Mid-Western Collegiate	317-237-5622
Missouri Valley	314-421-0339
North Star	312-341-8549
Ohio Valley	615-327-2557
Pacific Coast	714-261-2525
Pacific – 10	510-932-4411
South Eastern	205-252-7415
Southern	704-255-7872
Southland	214-424-4833
Southwest	214-634-7353

Southwestern	504-523-7573
Sunbelt	813-872-1511
Trans America	404-548-3369
West Coast	415-751-9190
Western Athletic	303-795-1962
Yankee	617-353-4630

Professionalism

Once you are considered a professional your college eligibility is gone. You are a "professional" if you:

1. Are paid (in any form) or accept the promise of pay for participating in an athletics contest;
2. Sign a contract or verbally commit with an agent or a professional sports organization;
3. Request that your name be placed on a draft list or otherwise agree to negotiate with a professional sports organization;
4. Use your athletic skill for pay in any form (for example, TV commercials, demonstrations);
5. Play on a professional athletics team, or
6. Participate on an amateur sports team and receive, directly or indirectly, any salary, incentive payment, award, gratuity, educational expenses or expense allowances other than actual and necessary travel, and room and board expenses for practice and games.

Before enrolling in college you may:

1. Tryout (practice but not participate against outside competition) with a professional sports team at your own expense;

We are always tempted to reach the top and in sports the professional ranks are usually it. Turning pro means never returning to collegiate competition in that sport. For some like football star Raghib Ismail from Notre Dame pro football was worth not finishing college. For the majority I urge you to finish college first and weigh your options with a degree in your back pocket.

2. Receive actual and necessary expenses from any professional sports organizations for one visit per professional organization not in excess of 48 hours.

3. Receive a fee for teaching a lesson in a particular sport.

Please, if you are unsure, contact the NCAA office in Kansas to answer your questions prior to accepting any monies.

Professional Agents

With all athletics we see the appearance of people who wish to represent promising athletes. The lure of big money contracts with pro teams and large advertising deals for athletes has created a need for professional advice. You could be in trouble with the NCAA if you agree to be represented by an agent while you are still in high school or college.

Accepting any gifts from an agent or player representative will jeopardize you college athletic eligibility in that sport. Be careful. Talk to your family lawyer or your director of athletics first if you have a concern. Don't jeopardize a 4 year degree for an agent's flashy gift. Your talents will pay for themselves many times after graduation.

Most of the young professional athletes I spoke with selected their agents based on referrals from other associates already playing in that sport. The agents will take a generous cut from your earnings in return for a better contract. There are good and bad agents. Look for the best player you know and ask him/her who they deal with to begin your search.

CHAPTER 3

Recruiting – Am I a Blue Chipper?

COLLEGE COACHES HAVE a very simple rating level for prospective athletes. At the top of this chart is what they refer to as a "blue chipper." This word is borrowed from the stock market where a blue chip stock is one which is a quality, long term, sound investment. Obviously, it is the scout and coach's job to obtain as many blue chip players as possible. An average is about 4 per year per college. This depends on the sport. Obviously more recruits are needed for football than baseball or basketball.

The next level is simply the second level "chippers". These are the players who get the scholarships after the blue chippers have selected a college. These candidates are also actively recruited by colleges and often these athletes turn out to be real success stories.

The third level is the "walkons." These individuals may have received mass mailings by a few colleges but have not been actively recruited. They choose to enroll at a school of their own choice without any admission help from the athletic department. In both of the first two categories each coach presents a "preference list" which is closely examined by the admissions department to assist with the candidate's admission to the college. The "walkon" is a student athlete who has to beat out someone who has either been given a scholarship already or is receiving special financial assistance. The "walkon's" chances to make the varsity squad are generally poor; however, each year there are a few major surprises in college training camps.

My advice, to any athlete who feels that he is a candidate for a college program, is to sit tight and take your time to learn about all of your options. If the U.S. college route is how you would like to proceed, contact the NCAA office and make sure you are an eligible player. For instance, any player with greater than 48 hours of playing exposure at the major junior 'A' level is ineligible to compete in NCAA hockey.

If you are a top recruit (blue chipper) you probably, but not always, have received mail and questionnaires since you were in grade eleven. Because of NCAA rules, which were discussed earlier, this is all the coaches are allowed to do prior to a candidate entering his senior year in high school. Coaches can say "hello" to a player and "nice game" but the regulations, as discussed earlier, are quite strict to prevent them from discussing the college's program prior to the senior year of high school.

When senior year arrives, the Division I and II prospects receive many letters from coaches. Players who are candidates for Division III are also mailed out extensive packages.

What does a candidate do next? In most cases he should visit a campus. At Division I and II schools and those with specific athletic scholarships, a paid visit is offered by the coach. The NCAA rules prohibit any high school senior from taking more than five visits at the expense of the school. A visit includes paid flight, meals and mileage. The length of the visit can only be 48 hours. The visit will be one of seeing a game, visiting the college facilities, perhaps meeting a few players and always a look at the social life available.

If a coach says he wants you to visit his campus and stay overnight his intentions are serious. The next step, after the 'wining and dining' is the weekly contact by an assistant coach or perhaps a visit to your home. In the Division III schools usually only telephone contact is made.

The Duke Medical Center is widely recognized as one of the world's finest health-care and research facilities. (Courtesy of Duke University.)

Harvard.
(Photo by Tim Morse. Courtesy of Harvard Univesrsity.)

The coach's next step after he has established continuous communications with a prospect is to offer full scholarship, or a partial scholarship and financial aid package. At the Ivy League schools and smaller NESCAC schools the coach can only state that the candidate would be a true four year starter. The financial aid office, after receiving your application, makes an assistance proposal to you.

The larger name schools, such as Boston College, Duke University, Stanford and Michigan State have larger recruiting budgets and you must keep this in mind. The smaller colleges also actively recruit, but it is the quality of education and the competitive athletic programs that they use as their selling vehicle. At schools like Bowdoin College (Maine), Colby College (Maine), Amherst (Mass.) and Hamilton (N.Y.) are members of NESCAC (The New England Small College Athletic Conference) the recruiting rules are very strict. They are not even allowed to print the names of their recruits in the newspaper. The reason for this is that these schools are academic institutions first and foremost.

CHAPTER 4

Selecting a College

THE MOST IMPORTANT thing to keep in mind when selecting a college is 'fit'. Just like you would not purchase a new pair of sneakers without the proper sizing, some colleges will not fit into your goals.

One of the biggest decisions is to decide if you would rather attend a larger campus (over 10,000 full time students) like Michigan State or Ohio State or one of the two smaller sizes. The medium size school (eg. Harvard, Yale) is the next option with a 5,000 to 10,000 total student population. In these schools, the incoming freshman class is usually in the 2,000 student range. The last category is the small, usually private, college, with a 1,000 to 5,000 student campus which includes an incoming freshman class of 350 to 600 students (eg. Colgate University, Hamilton College).

A larger campus will have many advantages because of its size. Usually better recreational activities are available. These schools are often located in larger cities which may allow for greater athletic exposure to showcase an athlete's skills. However, scholastically, you will find these schools will have very large class sizes. They will, perhaps, allow a student a larger choice of introductory courses at more convenient times but introductory courses of over 700 people are common. These large classes allow little class interaction or personal contact with professors. Large colleges have some big name professors, but trying to see them on a one to one basis is usually difficult. Teaching assistants (graduate students) often end up as the only avenue for assistance with questions. The larger schools do offer fantastic opportunities to the independent individual.

The smaller colleges have the big advantage in academics. These campuses are perfect atmospheres for one-on-one learning. The reduced class sizes lead to a more personal learning environment. This is shown to be the largest selling point to prospective student athlete for small colleges. It is common at a school like Hamilton College, in Clinton N.Y., or a Williams College (Williams, Mass.) to be in a second year economics class with a class size of under twenty students.

In selecting your college, keep in mind the 'fish bowl' effect. Would you rather be a small fish in a big bowl or a big fish in a small bowl. A mediocre player who attends a large, Division I program and just barely makes it could probably be a four year starter at a smaller college and, perhaps elected captain in his senior year.

It is important to know your chances of playing at a college prior to your attending the school. The easiest way to determine this is to ask the prospective coach what your chances are. The coach will usually be frank with you and his advice is invaluable in evaluating your level of play. Often, these coaches are a close knit group of men and they have been known to pass a player's name on to another more suitable program.

A player shouldn't be worried about which program will give him offer the best exposure to professional athletics. If a player is good enough the scouts will find him. Each year, many Division I and II players make the step to the NHL, NFL, NBA and professional baseball. Each year more and more players are drafted from the American college ranks. Looking at pro rosters will quickly show numerous college backgrounds from Divisions I and II and occasionally Division III.

Duke's Danny Ferry goes to the hoop. Danny is now a successful business-man with a Duke dgree on his resume. (Courtesy of Duke University.)

The candidate must keep in mind that selecting a college is like four year marriage. The student must be compatible with the school academically, socially and, of course, with the athletic program. If one of these becomes a problem, a student's college career often will be greatly affected. These three areas are all closely related. Coaches are very quick to point out that many a student athlete has had unpleasant experiences when they let down on their book work to 'concentrate' on athletics. Others simply couldn't cope with the stress of studying for exams and practicing seven days a week. The student must keep in mind that he/she is there for an education first, to play college athletics second and then, and only then to socialize.

THE MAJOR COLLEGE SPORTS

Baseball
Basketball
Football
Hockey

Full-Ride or Partial Ride?

The NCAA maintains strict controls over the number of scholarships available in each sport it sponsors. It has an internal audit team that makes certain no college is guilty of violating the guideline. If a violation occurs stiff penalties are imposed.

With scholarships based solely on "athletic ability" each sport has restrictions. In men's football and basketball the NCAA refers to the amount of scholarships available as "head-count" sports. This means each Division I school can offer a total number only of students receiving full or partial aid. For Division I football in 1991-92 the total head count is 92. The NCAA will reduce the level to 88 in 1993-94 and to 85 in 1994-95.

For Division I basketball the head count is 14 in 1991-92. It will be reduced to 13 in 1993 and after.

Division by division analysis is contained in the individual sport analysis following.

Division II football has a limit of 40 "equivalency scholarships." Which means two people might get a 50% scholarship each. Together these two make up one (1) equivalency scholarship. The percentage can be any combination of 100%.

Division II basketball has an equivalency scholarship limit of 12 created on the same basis.

Criteria for Academic Ranking Scores

The academic rating which follows is based on an analysis of the scores achieved by entrance level freshmen on the SAT and or ACT tests. The Peterson's Guide to Four-Year Colleges, 1991 was my reference manual for this evaluation. There are 5 major categories:

1. Toughest colleges/universities to get into: ***** (5 star rating). In this category more than 75% of the freshmen or first year entrants were in the top 10% of their high school class. These individuals also scored over 1,250 on the combined verbal and mathematical SAT. In some cases they could have scored a 29 on the ACT. These institutions accepted 30% or fewer applicants.

2. Quite tough to get into: **** (4 star). This rating will encompass a group of colleges where 50% of the freshmen were in the top 10% of their high school class and scored over 1,150 on the SAT and/or 26 on the ACT. Here schools reported accepting 60% or lower of incoming applicants.

3. Some difficulty to get into: *** (3 star). Here, three stars indicate schools where 75% of the freshmen were in the top half of their high schools graduating class. They also scored over 900 on the SAT or over 18 on the ACT.

   The acceptance rate increases significantly to approximately 85% of all incoming applications.

4. Little difficulty to get into: ** (2 star). Up to 95% of applicants are accepted.

5. Any graduate will do category: * (1 star). As long as you graduate from high school you are in. I question the value of a degree here.

BASEBALL

The sport of baseball competes at all three NCAA levels or divisions. There are NCAA national champions for each category. Traditionally baseball programs with the greatest success in competing for the NCAA championships in Division I have been located in the Southern U.S. The site for the championship in Division I each year since 1950 has been Omaha, Nebraska. The school who has won the most College World Series (as the NCAA Division I championship is referred) is the University of Southern California with 11 championships since the 1947 inception of the College World Series.

Other schools with successful baseball histories are; Stanford, Arizona, Arizona State, Cal St. Fullerton, Wichita State, Louisiana State, Georgia and Texas.

In 1991, the winner of the College World Series was Louisiana State with a 4-0 record. The Louisiana State Tigers hit .329 in the tournament and set two NCAA College World Series records. Their top pitcher was Chad Ogea and they were led by the batting of Johnny Tellechea with a .438 in 16 at bats. In 1991, 7 LSU Tigers signed professional baseball contracts. They are:

Gary Hymel (C)	Montreal Expos
Lyle Mouton (OF)	New York Yankees
Chad Ogea (P)	Cleveland Indians
Paul Byrd (P)	Cleveland Indians
Mark LaRosa (P)	Montreal Expos
Luis Garcia (3B)	Minnesota Twins
Rich Cordani (OF)	Milwaukee Brewers

Since 1984, the LSU Tigers coached by Skip Bertman have had 45 players who have signed professional baseball contracts.

In 1991, second place went to Wichita State at (3-1), third to Creighton (2-1), fourth to Florida (2-1) and fifth to Fresno State at (1-2).

Division I – Baseball Best Picks

The schools that offer the best baseball environment coupled with a good to excellent learning environment and the best exposure to the pro circuit are:

SCHOOL	Tournament Record Since 1947	Number of Scholarships NCCA	Academic Rating
1. Southern California	.741	11	***
2. Arizona State	.739	11	***
3. Arizona	.621	11	***
4. Cal St. Fullerton	.620	11	***
5. California	.722	11	***
6. Georgia	.706	11	***
7. Texas	.667	11	***
8. Wichita State	.643	11	*
9. Stanford	.663	11	*****
10. Michigan	.614	11	*****
11. Minnesota	.547	11	****
12. Clemson	.527	11	***
13. Creighton	.571	11	***
14. Long Beach State	.750	11	***
15. Fresno State	.481	11	***
16. Florida	.519	11	**
17. St. John's (N.Y.)	.522	11	**

18. Mississippi	.558	11	**
19. Southern Illinois	.565	11	**
20. Missouri	.544	11	**

At the college level baseball, although not having the huge national television contracts of football or basketball, has recently begun to receive more media coverage and hence better national recognition. It has become an excellent incubator for many top high school prospects not wanting to gamble on directly entering the multiple level minor league systems of the professional club organizations.

Many top high school draftees are opting for spending some developmental time in the college ranks. The college coaches are generally very strong on stressing the basics and putting tremendous importance on the fundamentals of baseball. Generally skill development is very strong. College baseball allows younger players, slower to develop, time to mature physically and mentally. In all, the collegiate baseball programs are an ideal breeding ground in molding professional baseball prospects.

Division II – Baseball Best Picks

Division II schools by attendance have generally lower numbers of students and complete logically at a level below the major Division I programs. That is not to say all Division II schools could not compete at the Division I playing level. For national championship reasons categories were created to place teams from similar types of institutions into a fair playing structure.

Again, with Division II baseball programs, the best colleges athletically are found in the Southern U.S. In 1991, Jacksonville State (4-1) behind pitcher Tim VanEgmund (2-0) and an 0.98 ERA won its second straight Division II championship. In the team standings the top 5 finishers were:

1. Jacksonville State
2. Mo. Southern State

3. U.C. Riverside
4. Longwood
5. Florida Southern

The top 20 best picks are below.

Ranking	School	NCCA Tournament Record	Academic Score
1	Cal Poly, Pomona, CA.	.711	**
3	Fla. Southern, FA.	.690	**
5	Troy St., AL	.691	**
2	U.C., Riverside, CA.	.692	***
4	Univ. of New Haven, CT.	.621	**
6	Jacksonville State, FL.	.594	**
7	Le Moyne, N.Y.	.510	***
8	Columbus, Ohio	.528	***
9	Delta State, M.S.	.554	**
10	Chapman	.579	***
11	SIU – Edwardsburg	.521	**
12	Armstrong State, GA.	.444	**
13	Shippensburg, Univ. of Penn.	.429	***
14	Cal State Univ. Northridge	.622	***
15	Cal State, Sacramento	.462	***
16	Tampa College, FA.	.486	**
17	Longwood College, VA.	.526	
18	Univ. of Mo., St. Louis	.553	***
19	Valdosta St., GA	.609	**
20	Lewis Univ., IL.	.553	***

Division III

In 1991, the University of Southern Maine defeated Trenton State 9-0 to win its first NCAA Division III National Championship. They finished the tournament at (4-0) with 42 runs.

Division III baseball like all other Division III sports must rely on attracting students/athletes because of its small classes and generally low professor-student learning ratios. With fewer distractions many Division III students perform very well and are excellent post graduate- candidates. All Division III schools cannot offer athletic scholarships and all assistance financially is done by complying with the requirements needed to qualify for financial aid.

Most Division III colleges seem to be of smaller size in student population generally less than 3,000 students.

The top 10 picks based on recent NCAA success since the championships began in 1976 are:

School	NCCA Winning %	Number of Equivalency Scholarships Available	Academic Score
1. Marietta College	.719	All based on OH financial aid packages	***
2. Cal St., Staniskus	.700		**
3. Glassboro State, N.J.	.700		***
4. Wis-Oshkosh, WIS.	.674		***
5. Cal St.	.667		***
6. Ithaca College, NY	.632		***
7. Eastern Conn. St.	.615		***
8. N.C. Wesleyan, N.C.	.612		***
9. Univ. of S. Maine	.516		***
10. Trenton St., N.J.	.516		**

BASKETBALL

The sport of basketball has become one of the big money sports for hundreds of colleges across America. With revenues from television and radio, colleges enjoy a huge influx of monies from successful basketball programs. As a result, basketball programs are run extremely professionally for amateur athletes. High school student athletes with basketball promise are recruited heavily, usually by many schools. Basketball players who compete at the Division I level have several choices available upon graduation. They can, of course, enter the work force. If they have been good players alumni supporters have been known to eagerly assist in gaining employment for the student. Professional basketball in Europe and Asia has become the home for many collegians in recent years. Salaries are very appealing there. The NBA, unlike the larger participation sports of football and hockey, require fewer starters or backup players and subsequently fewer collegians jump directly into the NBA to earn their livings.

Division I

In basketball we see three strong Divisions of play; I, II, and III. Division I NCAA Championships began in 1939. Basketball is one of the oldest collegiate sports.

In 1991, Duke University won its first NCAA Championship defeating Kansas. Duke repeated again in 1992. Duke has been a regular in NCAA finals and a member of the famed final four 10 times.

The top 20 basketball programs based in recent (past 10 years) NCAA tournament success and the academic environment are:

Rank	School	NCCA Winning %	Number of Head Count Scholarships	Academic Record
1	Seton Hall, N.J.	.750	14	***
2	UCLA	.747	14	****
3	Duke, N.C.	.746	14	*****
4	Indiana	.732	14	***
5	Nevada, Las Vegas	.732	14	***
6	Kansas State Univ.	.677	14	*
7	Univ. of North Carolina	.675	14	***
8	Univ. of Michigan	.675	14	*****
9	North Carolina St.	.659	14	***
10	Georgetown Univ. D.C.	.659	14	*****
11	Oklahoma St Univ., OK	.654	14	***
12	Michigan St.	.652	14	***
13	Univ. of Kentucky	.646	14	***
14	Ohio State	.636	14	*
15	Univ. of Oklahoma, Louisville	.623	14	***
16	Villanova	.608	14	****
17	Virginia	.600	14	****
18	Georgia Tech.	.600	14	****
19	Brigham Young, Utah	.600	14	***
20	Clemson Univ., S.C.	.600	14	***

Division II

Like other sports, in basketball we see good competition levels at the Division II level. The colleges tend to play at a lower athletic skill level than Division I. Most colleges also have lower attendance levels then the more recognized Division I schools. Division II schools, for the most part, do not have the benefit of large television contracts and their supporting revenues. They do offer scholarships based on athletics.

Division II basketball competition began in 1957. Until 1976 the NCAA Division II Championship was held in Evansville, Indianna. Since then, Springfield, Mass. is the tournament home. No one school has dominated over the years. Wesleyan College in Kentucky has the most championships at 5.

The top 20 schools based on their performance in the last 10 years and their academic reputation are found below.

Rank	School	NCCA Division II Winning %	Number of Equivalency Scholarships	Academic Record
1	North Alabama	.793	12	*
2	Kentucky Wesleyan College	.786	12	***
3	Univ. South Dakota	.750	12	***
4	Southeast Missouri State	.667	12	**
5	Florida Southern College	.659	12	***
6	South Dakota State	.659	12	***
7	Jacksonville State	.636	12	***
8	Wright State, Ohio	.632	12	*
9	Cheyney Univ. of Penn.	.627	12	**
10	New Hampton College	.615	12	**

11	North Dakota State	.610	12	*
12	Cal State, Bakersfield	.607	12	***
13	Missouri State, St. Louis	.600	12	***
14	Sacred Heart Univ. CT.	.595	12	***
15	Mt. St. Mary's, Maryland	.595	12	***
16	UC, Riverside	.595	12	****
17	Bridgeport State	.581	12	***
18	Assumption College, MA	.577	12	***
19	Virginia Union Univ.		12	**
20	Millersville Univ.	.556	12	***

Division III

In Division III we see much smaller basketball programs. This is due mainly to the small school attendance in most colleges. Competition level is actually quite good. You can see a very small private college, like Hamilton College in Clinton, N.Y. beat the more recognized Colgate University on a regular basis. At this level, don't let the fact that the college has an unfamiliar name enter into your evaluation of their basketball program. We must also recognize that their is an association of private colleges that specifically prevent their athletic teams from competing at the NCAA level past a specific date in the school year. This association is called NESCAC, New England Small college Athletic Conference. The colleges tend to have very high standards and they have created this ruling to protect the academic standard. The members at present are; Amherst College (Mass.), Bowdoin College (Maine), Colby College (Maine), Hamilton College (N.Y.), Middlebury (Vermont), Wesleyan (CT), Bates (Mass), Connecticut College, Trinity College, Williams (Mass.), Tufts (Mass.).

None of the above highly selective academic colleges can compete in the NCAA Division III yearly championships.

In 1991, the NCAA Division III Champion was the Wisconsin — Platteville Pioneers. This was their first NCAA Championship. NCAA Division III Championships began in 1975. The team with the most championships is the University of Wisconsin at Whitewater with 3 national wins in recent years.

The top 10 schools for Division III, excluding *all* NESCAC colleges are found below.

Rank	School	NCCA Winning %	Number of Equivalency Scholarships	Academic Rank
1	North Park College, IL.	.813	Financial aid only	***
2	University of Wisconsin- Whitewater	.762		***
3	Potsdam State, NY	.750		***
4	Rochester, NY (Only 3 years competition)	.833		*** ***
5	LeMoyne - Owen	.750		***
6	Wittenberg	.689		*
7	Uni. of Scranton, PA	.658		***
8	Clark (Mass.)	.656		*
9	Augustana (Ill.)	.652		***
10	Nebraska Wesleyan University	.630		***

Other NESCAC Basketball programs with excellent education but unable to compete because of academic restrictions in national tournaments are:

1. Hamilton College, (Clinton, N.Y.) ****
2. Middlebury College, (Vermont) ****
3. Williams College, (Mass.) *****

FOOTBALL

The highest level of play for collegiate football is Division I-A. The NCAA does not sponsor a Division I-A National Championship. The Division I-A National Champion is selected by a polling system. The polling system is based upon the voters' analysis

The national polls include A.P. (Associated Press) Poll which is a media poll made up of writers and broadcasters. The U.P.I. (United Press International) poll is made from coaches only from Division I-A schools. Since 1982, there has been a U.S.A. Today/Cable News Network Poll compiled by and from key media people.

The U.S.A. Today people also now run the U.P.I. poll calculations for the U.P.I. organization. These 3 polls are weekly polls released continually throughout the football season. There is a fourth national football poll called the Football Writers of America Association Poll. This poll is released only at the conclusion of the season. The association awards their own national trophy called the Grantland Rice Trophy. In 1991 the University of Washington received this award.

It is difficult to get all the national polls to agree. In fact, you have to go back to 1964 to find an agreement selection of Alabama as national Champion. In most years the A.P. poll disagrees with the U.P.I. and USA Today polls. For example, in 1990 the U.P.I. poll selected Georgia Tech as the Division I-A Champion but the A.P. poll selected Colorado as the number one team. In 1991 we saw again the selection of co-winners with the University of Miami of Florida and the University of Washington being selected.

Division I-A football, for the reason of a lack of a formal NCAA tournament competition, has what is called a "Mythical National Champion". The selection each year is based not only on a college's win-loss record.

Probably your first exposure to college sports is through televised collegiate football. Football at the Division I-A level is simply enormous. Televised games fill millions of North American homes each season for several months of continued entertainment. With the large mass appeal we see the most substantial operating budgets of all NCAA athletics. Many colleges are able to finance their entire athletic programs through proceeds gained from well run football programs. In recent years funding has been given from big name football programs to the college's general academic budgets. Now, we see library's and other important academic areas beginning to benefit slowly from football success on the field. This is a fantastic sign.

The majority of games on television are played between Division I-A teams. These are schools like; Notre Dame, Michigan, University of Miami Florida, Penn State to name only a few. Since there is not an NCAA tournament second to rely on for a ranking of the collegiate football success we will have to use the college polls as our basis.

The NCAA Division I-A level produces an enormous talent base from which the NFL, CFL and various semi-pro leagues draw. Some examples of recent Division I-A college players who have gone on to the pros are below.

PLAYER	COLLEGE	PRO TEAM
Jim McMahon	Brighham Young	Philadelphia
Steve Young	Brighham Young	Philadelphia
Vinny Testaverde	Miami	Miami
Troy Alkman	Oklahoma / UCLA	Dallas
John Elway	Stanford	Denver
Bernie Kosar	Miami	Cinncinatti
Dan Marino	Pittsburg	Miami
Raghib Ismail	Notre Dame	Toronto

The top 30 schools based on all-time NCAA Division 1-A team won-lost records and academic ranking follow below.

Rank	School	Number of Head Count Scholarships*	NCCA Winning %	Academic Rank
1	Notre Dame	92	.759	*****
2	Michigan	92	.743	*****
3	Alabama	92	.728	***
4	Oklahoma	92	.722	***
5	Texas	92	.716	***
6	Southern Cal.	92	.709	***
7	Ohio St.	92	.700	*
8	Penn St.	92	.688	****
9	Nebraska	92	.686	***
10	Tennessee	92	.684	****
11	Central Michigan	92	.650	***
12	Army	92	.642	****
13	Louisiana St.	92	.641	***
14	Miami (Ohio)	92	.637	****
15	Arizona St.	92	.635	***
16	Washington	92	.630	***
17	Georgia	92	.630	***
18	Auburn	92	.618	***
19	Florida St.	92	.617	***
20	Michigan St.	92	.616	***
21	Minnesota	92	.615	***
22	Colorado	92	.606	***

23	Arkansas	92	.605	*
24	UCLA	92	.602	****
25	Pittsburg	92	.601	***
26	Georgia Tech.	92	.599	****
27	Tulsa	92	.597	***
28	Bowling Green	92	.596	***
29	Southern Miss.	92	.596	**
30	Fresno St.	92*	.595	***

* This limit will reduce in 1993-94 to 88 and to 85 in 1994-95. The National Champion is decided by the poll rankings as discussed earlier. Some recent examples of final year-end rankings are below.

The AP Associated Press Final Poll

1988 TEAM
1.	Notre Dame
2.	Miami (Fla.)
3.	Florida St.
4.	Michigan
5.	West Va.
6.	UCLA
7.	Southern Cal.
8.	Auburn
9.	Clemson
10.	Nebraska
11.	Oklahoma St.
12.	Arkansas

13.	Syracuse
14.	Oklahoma
15.	Georgia
16.	Washington St.
17.	Alabama
18.	Houston
19.	Louisiana St.
20.	Indiana

1989 TEAM	
1.	Miami (Fla.)
2.	Notre Dame
3.	Florida St.
4.	Colorado
5.	Tennessee
6.	Auburn
7.	Michigan
8.	Southern Cal.
9.	Alabama
10.	Illinois
11.	Nebraska
12.	Clemson
13.	Arkansas
14.	Houston
15.	Penn St.
16.	Michigan St.
17.	Pittsburgh

18.	Virginia
19.	Texas Tech.
20.	Texas A & M

1990 TEAM	
1.	Colorado
2.	Georgia Tech.
3.	Miami (Fla.)
4.	Florida St.
5.	Washington
6.	Notre Dame
7.	Michigan
8.	Tennessee
9.	Clemson
10.	Houston
11.	Penn St.
12.	Texas
13.	Florida
14.	Louisville
15.	Texas A & M
16.	Michigan St.
17.	Oklahoma
18.	Iowa
19.	Auburn
20.	Southern Cal.

The United Press International (Coaches) Poll

1988 TEAM
1. Notre Dame
2. Miami (Fla.)
3. Florida St.
4. Michigan
5. West Va.
6. UCLA
7. Auburn
8. Clemson
9. Southern Cal.
10. Nebraska
11. Oklahoma St.
12. Syracuse
13. Arkansas
14. Oklahoma
15. Georgia
16. Washington St.
17. North Carolina
18. Alabama
19. Indiana
20. Wyoming

1989 TEAM
1. Miami (Fla.)
2. Florida St.
3. Notre Dame

4.	Colorado
5.	Tennessee
6.	Auburn
7.	Alabama
8.	Michigan
9.	Southern Cal.
10.	Illinois
11.	Clemson
12.	Nebraska
14.	Penn St.
15.	Virginia
16.	Texas Tech.
17.	Michigan St.
18.	Brigham Young
19.	Pittsburgh
20.	Washington

1990 TEAM	
1.	Georgia Tech.
2.	Colorado
3.	Miami (Fla.)
4.	Florida St.
5.	Washington
6.	Notre Dame
7.	Tennessee
8.	Michigan
9.	Clemson

10.	Penn St.
11.	Texas
12.	Louisville
13.	Texas A & M
14.	Michigan St.
15.	Virginia
16.	Iowa
17.	Brigham Young
18.	Nebraska
19.	Auburn
20.	San Jose St.

The USA Today/Cable News Network Poll (Since 1982)

	1988 TEAM
1.	Notre Dame
2.	Miami (Fla.)
3.	Florida St.
4.	UCLA
5.	Michigan
6.	West Va.
7.	Southern Cal.
8.	Nebraska
9.	Auburn
10.	Clemson
11.	Oklahoma St.
12.	Syracuse
13.	Oklahoma

14.	Arkansas
15.	Washington St.
16.	Georgia
17.	Alabama
18.	North Caro. St.
19.	Houston
20.	Indiana
21.	Wyoming
22.	Louisiana St.
23.	Colorado
24.	Southern Miss.
25.	Brigham Young

1989 TEAM	
1.	Miami (Fla.)
2.	Notre Dame
3.	Florida St.
4.	Colorado
5.	Tennessee
6.	Auburn
7.	Southern Cal.
8.	Michigan
9.	Alabama
10.	Illinois
11.	Nebraska
12.	Clemson
13.	Arkansas

14.	Houston
15.	Penn St.
16.	Virginia
17.	Michigan St.
18.	Texas Tech.
19.	Pittsburgh
20.	Texas A & M
21.	West Va.
22.	Brigham Young
23.	Syracuse
24.	Ohio St.
25.	Washington

1990 TEAM	
1.	Colorado
2.	Georgia Tech.
3.	Miami (Fla.)
4.	Florida St.
5.	Washington
6.	Notre Dame
7.	Tennessee
8.	Michigan
9.	Clemson
10.	Texas
11.	Penn St.
12.	Houston
13.	Florida

14.	Louisville
15.	Michigan
16.	Texas A & M
17.	Oklahoma
18.	Iowa
19.	Auburn
20.	Brigham Young
21.	Mississippi
22.	Southern Cal.
23.	Nebraska
24.	Illinois
25.	Virginia

Football – Division I-AA

Division 1-AA colleges play at a level just below the larger budgeted football programs of the Division I-A. These colleges generally do not receive televised contracts of significance. They are also generally operating on much smaller budgets. Their programs are thus forced to function as a much tighter ship. This affects the number of scholarships they can offer and also the levels of operating expenses their programs can support. This is not to say the quality of players suffers dramatically. Several top name NFL players have graduated from Division I-AA programs. Some recent examples are; Neil Lomax (St. Louis Cardinals), John Freese (San Diego), Gill Fenerty (New Orleans). We can also see graduates John Taylor of Delaware State University and Jerry Rice of Mississippi Valley State University playing key roles in the NFL. Several players from this division have also gone on to successful careers in the CFL.

The NCAA Division I-AA National Championship began in 1978.

Georgia Southern University has won the title the most times with four. Eastern Kentucky University is next two NCAA Championships. In 1991, Youngstown State won their first title after placing second in the polls in 1990 and fourteenth in the polls in 1989.

The top 15 programs for Division I-A based on NCAA tournament appearances winning percentages (last 10 years) as well as academic reputation are found below:

Rank	School	NCCA Winning %	Number of Head Count Scholarships*	Academic Rank
1.	Georgia Southern Univ. (GA)	.909	92	***
2.	Boise State	.625	92	**
3.	Furman Univ. (SC)	.625	92	****
4.	Arkansas St.	.600	92	**
5.	Eastern Kentucky	.591	92	**
6.	Nevada - Reno	.571	92	**
7.	Northern Iowa	.500	92	**
8.	Middle Tenn. State	.500	92	**
9.	Delaware State College (DE)	.429	92	***
10.	Eastern Ill. Univ.	.429	92	***
11.	Appalachian State Univ. (N.C.)	.400	92	***
12.	Youngstown State	.400	92	*
13.	Univ. of Idaho	.364	92	***
14.	Stephen F. Austin State Univ. (Texas) (only 2 years NCAA competition)	.667	92	***
15.	Northeast Louisiana State Univ (only 2 years NCAA competition)	.800	92	*

Division II – Football

Division II football programs are widely spread across the nation geographically. This division has produced numerous student athletes who have gone on to the professional ranks in both the NFL and in the CFL.

The most successful college program in recent years has been the North Dakota State Bisons. In 1990, they won their fifth NCAA Division II football championship in the last eight years.

The NCAA began its national Division II Championship in 1973. Prior to this date four regional bowl games were played to create a final champion.

The site of the championship for Division II has been Florence, Alabama since 1986. This site has just received an extension to host the NCAA finals until 1994. Because of the smaller attendance for Division II football a fixed site has proven more economically viable to host the championship.

Some familiar ex-student athletes from the Division II ranks are found below;

PLAYER	PRO TEAM	COLLEGE TEAM
Terry Bradshaw	Pittsburgh Steelers Louisiana Tech. (now Division I)	
Billy "White Shoes" Johnson	Denver Broncos Montreal (CFL)	Widner Univ.
Jim Zorn	Seattle, Green Bay	Cal Poly Ponoma
John Bailey	Chicago Bears	Texas A & I
Heath Sherman	Philadelphia Eagles	Texas A & I

The top 15 programs for Division II based on NCAA tournament appearances winning percentages (last 10 years) and academic reputation are found below:

Rank	School	NCCA Winning %	Number of Equivalency Scholarships*	Academic Rank
1.	North Dakota St.	.806	40	*
2.	Mississippi College	.700	40	***
3.	Troy State (3 yrs.), Alabama	.875	40	**
4.	Portland State	.667	40	**
5.	Cal Poly SLO	.667	40	***
6.	Indiana Univ. of Penn	.556	40	***
7.	Jacksonville State Alabama	.500	40	*
8.	Univ. of North Alabama	.500	40	*
9.	Northern Michigan Univ.	.500	40	**
10.	Angelo State Univ. (Texas)	.500	40	***
11.	Univ. of South Dakota	.500	40	***
12.	Texas A & I	.500	40	***
13.	Central St. (Ohio)	.429	40	*
14.	Virginia Union Univ. (VA)	.308	40	**
15.	Winston-Salem State Univ. (NC)	.200	40	**

* The NCAA will reduce the number of head count scholarships in 1993 to 88 and 1994 to 85 in Division I Football.

Football – Division III

As we discussed earlier, Division III athletic programs cannot offer scholarships based on athletic ability. Here, we see generally athletes who decide to play football strictly for the love of the game. The colleges do often offer various financial aid

Division III Allegheny Coolege. Tail back Stanley Drayton, NCAA Division III scoring Champion, 1991 (Courtesy of Allegheny College.)

packages to lure incoming student athletes. However, here budgets are very small in comparison to the other Divisions. Attendance at Division I contests may reach 100,000 people at a Michigan State game. Attendance at Division III football games usually is in the 1,000 to 3,000 range. The football is played at a good skill level with limited coaching staffs and player rosters.

The professional scouts do attend some games but generally the route to the pro ranks is a long shot. There have been exceptions. Dave Crieg has been the quarterback with Seattle Seahawks for about 10 years. Dave attended Mitton College back in the early 1980's. Milton has since discontinued its football program. Jeff Ouery played his college ball with Millikin University in Illinois. Jeff now plays for the Green Bay Packers.

Occasionally, we see Division III student athletes rising to the pro ranks because they are late bloomers developing much later than the higher profile recruits sought after in high school by the big name colleges. Sometimes we see an athlete who has changed sports from track to football late in his collegiate career. One example recently was Tom Newberry from the University of Wisconsin. Tom played Lacrosse at college but was recruited because of his size and quickness to play offensive lineman for the Los Angeles Rams of the NFL.

In 1990 Allegheney College won its first NCAA title for Division III football. They beat Lycoming College in the finals. The NCAA has held an NCAA championship since 1973. Augustana College has won the crown four times. The host site has been Phoenix City, Alabama, fifteen times with the championship moving to Bradenton, Florida since 1990.

The top 15 college programs based on NCAA winning percentage in the last ten years and academic reputation are found below.

Rank	School	NCCA Winning %	Scholarships*	Academic Rank
1.	Augustona College (Ill.)	.731	Financial aid Packages only	***
2.	Allegheny College PA (only 2 years)	.800		***
3.	Wittenberg Univ. (Ohio)	.769		***
4.	Ithaca (N.Y)	.708		***
5.	Central University of Iowa	.652		***
6.	Univ. of Dayton, Ohio	.650		***
7.	Widener University, PA	.643		***
8.	Saint John's Univ. Minn.	.600		***
9.	Lycoming College, PA	.571		***
10.	Union College (N.Y.)	.545		****
11.	Salisbury St. Univ., MD (only 3 years)	.625		***
12.	Wagner College, N.Y.	.571		***
13.	Montclair St. College, N.J.	.500		***
14.	Ferrum College (VA)	.500		***
15.	Washington & Jefferson College (PA)	.375		***

HOCKEY

Ice hockey is one of the oldest NCAA competitions. Division I hockey originally started back in 1948. The original tournament site was Colorado Springs. Ice hockey has come a long way since then. Programs today produce a great number of talented sound hockey players. The NHL and the European professional leagues actively recruit players from Division I programs. Scouts find the players more mature than those right out of high schools or junior A hockey.

The NCAA Division I crown has been won the most times by the University of Michigan with seven titles. In recent years Wisconsin and North Dakota each have two national titles. No one team has dominated the championship since the early 1980's. In 1991, the host site for the highly attended tournament was St. Paul, Minnesota. As in recent years the final game was very close with Northern Michigan needing triple overtime to beat Boston University 8-7. Attendance was generally well over 10,000 for each tournament game. There are some televised games generating small revenues to selected colleges.

The top 20 schools in ice hockey based on NCAA tournament winning percentage and academic reputation are listed below.

Rank	School	NCCA Winning %	Maximum Number of Equivalency Scholarships*	Academic Rank
1	University of Michigan	.719	20	*****
2	University of Wisconsin	.694	20	***
3	University of North Dakota	.667	20	*
4	University of Denver	.654	20	***

5	Michigan Tech.	.625	20	***
6	University of Minnesota – Twin Cities	.611	20	***
7	Northern Michigan Univ.	.571	20	**
8	Michigan State University	.557	20	***
9	Rensselaer Poly Tech. Institute	.536	20	****
10	Boston University	.535	20	***
11	University of Maine	.500	20	***
12	Lake Superior State, MI	.500	20	***
13	University of Minnesota	.500	20	***
14	Colgate University	.500	20	****
15	Northeastern Univ., MA	.583	20	***
16	Cornell University	.476*		*****
17	Merimack College, MA (only 1 year)	.500	20	***
18	Clarkson Univ., N.Y.	.442	20	****
19	Harvard	.375*		*****
20	Boston College	.302	20	****

* Ivy League cannot offer athletic scholarships, only financial aid

In men's ice hockey Division II national competition has been eliminated. Colleges complete now at Division III level if they are not competing at the Division I level.

Division III hockey has become a much improved national championship since the elimination of the Division II trophy. Division II ended in 1984.

The most successful College at the Division III level is the University of Wisconsin at Stevens Point. Wisconsin won the title in 1991 for the third straight time which is a record.

The tournament was hosted by Elimira College in New York State. Division III hockey is generally played in approximately 2,500 seat arenas. The players are usually less talented than the Division I calibre. There has been some interest of late in scouting the division play from selected professional scouts. Televised games are rare. These colleges run on much less expansive budgets than the Division I schools. As always, Division III programs also are not allowed to offer athletic scholarships. Financial aid packages are the only presentations available to incoming freshmen.

It should be noted again that athletic competition beyond March first is not allowed for any college who is a member of the New England Small College Athletic Conference. This presents some colleges with excellent records from competing at the NCAA tournament each year. NESCAC was created to place strict recruiting guidelines on its members. This is the New England Small College Athletic Conference. This conference was formed to make sure that all coaches follow the same recruiting principles. Guidelines state that academics must come first and athletics second. This conference does not even allow its members to participate in national play down after a specified date. It also does not allow more than 26 games to be played by any team in one season. Usually, November 1 is the first day allowed for a coach to run a practice. In summary, this conference was designed to protect the student athlete, allowing him to put his full efforts into his scholastic efforts.

The top 15 colleges based on their NCAA Division III winning percentages at tournament play and their academic reputation are found below.

Rank	School	NCCA Winning %	Scholarships*	Academic Rank
1	University of Wisconsin at Stevens Point	.763	Financial Aid Pkgs only	***
2	University of Wisconsin at River Falls	.778		***
3	Rochester Institute of Technology	.763		***
4	St. Cloud State, Minn.	.600		***
5	Bemidji State, Minn.	.571		***
6	Babson College	.516		****
7	Elmira College	.500		**
8	Monkato State, Minn.	.500		***
9	Plattsburg State (NY)	.538		***
10	Union College, NY	.375		****
11	Genesseo State, NY	.333		***
12	Mersyhurst College, P.A.	.333		***
13	Norwich University, V.T.	.333		***
14	Oswego State (N.Y.)	.286		***
15	Gust. Adolphus College, Minn.	250		****

Top 5 NESCAC Colleges also with excellent winning percentages in seasonal competition:

School	Scholarships	Academic Rank
Bowdoin College, Maine	Financial Aid packages only	****
Colby College, Maine	for all NESCAC colleges	****
Hamilton College, N.Y.		****
Middlebury College, V.T.		****
Williams College, Mass.		***

The members of NESCAC are:
  Hamilton College (NY)
  Bowdoin College (ME)
  Colby College (ME)
  Williams College (MA)
  Amherst College (MA)
  Connecticut College (CT)
  Middlebury (VT)
  Trinity (MA)
  Tufts (MA)
  Wesleyan (CT)

What Are My Chances to Play College Hockey?

To really understand the tremendous opportunities that exist to play competitive college hockey, we must examine the number of playing positions available on each team. In Canada alone there are approximately 700 playing positions. Some of these positions come with scholarship money and financial assistance based on academics and on individual finances.

When we examine the U.S. college and university spectrums we see far greater numbers of playing opportunities.

Division I

There are 48 schools. Each school requires 20 "dressed" players per team. The average squad size for Division I is about 30. A taxi-squad or junior varsity often exists at this level. Therefore, we have approximately 1,440 players.

Division II

Here the NCAA tells us there are 15 schools, with an average squad size of 32 players per team. Therefore there are 480 players at the Division II level. There is no national Division II NCAA competition in hockey.

Division III

Do not be fooled into thinking all of these schools have the lowest level of college hockey. The division ranking is in regards to their school attendance level, not playing level. There are many Division III schools which have far superior hockey programs to Division II and even some Division I schools.

In Division III, many schools will also have junior varsity teams as feeders to their number one program.

Division III has 60 schools; therefore 60 x 20, or 1,200 players. Division III also has approximately 20 schools supporting junior varsity teams; therefore we must add 20 x 15 players, or 300. This gives us:

1,200 varsity players
300 junior varsity players
1,500 playing positions

In total we find:

Div. I Varsity	1,440 junior varsity	500 approx.
Div. II Varsity	480	
Div. III Varsity	1,200 junior varsity	300
TOTAL	3,120	800

Approximate total of players participating in U.S. college competitive programs is 3,920.

Obviously, these numbers are large, but we must keep in mind that each team will have returning players. Since a college career only lasts four years graduating players are replaced by incoming freshmen. For each of these playing positions, players from across Canada and the United States will compete. The best advice is to go to the campus where your odds of starting in year one or two are the best. These odds, of course, depend on your skill level. Also, keep in mind you must have good grades in all cases to even be considered. In some cases you need excellent grades to be accepted into the college. If you are a player with above average grades in high school and good hockey skills, your chances are increased enormously. Each year hundreds of prospects for scholarships lose their opportunity to play competitive college hockey because of inadequate grades in high school.

For them the race is over, unless they choose to take what is called a "PG" year or post graduate year at a preparatory school (prep school). The number of positions open in these schools is limited. In a lot of cases a PG year has turned a athlete's attitude and grades around such that he then becomes an excellent scholarship candidate. On the next few pages you will find the addresses and telephone numbers for some of the better prep schools. These schools have become excellent feeder schools for many college programs, not only for hockey but also for other sports.

Prep schools are not only for PG students. They are sec-

McGill University, Montreal.
(Courtesy Magued Marcos, McGill Publications.)

ondary school institutions privately run much like a high school. They too have scholarship monies available and offer excellent learning environments.

Canadian University Associations

Canada, with a population of over 26 million, has a good number of high quality universities. Several rate with Harvard and Yale, others fall in a scale like many of the better colleges and still other schools rate academically like American state schools.

Although hockey comes to mind whenever athletics and Canada are mixed many other collegiate sports are played at good levels. Usually Canadian University hockey will compete at the Division I level. Basketball probably across the board at a Division III level. Track, swimming and football would fall between Division II and III in most comparisons. All of the schools listed sponsor several varsity sports. None offer full athletic scholarships since this is not allowed. Many individual provinces do offer significant financial assistance. It should be noted that the universities are much less expensive than American schools of similar calibre. All are heavily subsidized by the government.

Canadian schools offer financial assistance solely based on financial need. The individual provinces greatly subsidize tuition making them very reasonable.

Canadian Associations Varsity Level

SCHOOL	ACADEMIC RATING
CWUAA	
Calgary	***
Alberta	***
Manitoba	***
Saskatchewan	***
Brandon	***
Regina	***
Lethbridge	***
OUAA	
East Division	
Trois Rivieres	*
McGill	****
Concordia	***
Queen's	*****

RMC	****
Ottawa	***

Central Division

York	***
Western	****
Waterloo	***
Laurier	***
Toronto	****
Guelph	***

West Division

Brock	***
Ryerson	*****
Windsor	***
Laurentian	***
McMaster	*****

AUAA

McAdam Division

Moncton	***
U. PEI	***
St. Thomas	***
Mt. Allison	***
New Brunswick	***

Kelly Division

Acadia	***
St. Mary's	***

Cape Breton	**
Dalhousie	***
St. E. Xavier	***

35 Canadian Universities

Total 700 playing positions, many players graduate from Canadian Major Junior A and play Canadian University.

American Prep Schools With Hockey Programs
(In North East)
Schools marked with an asterisk (*) generally have produced more hockey candidates for Division I, II, and III in recent years.

Phillips Academy Andover, MA. 01810	617-475-3400 *
Avon Old Farms School Avon, CT. 06001	203-673-3201
Belmont Hill School Belmont, MA. 02178	617-484-4410
Berkshire School Sheffield, MA. 01257	413-229-8511 *
Berwick Academy South Berwick, Maine 03908	207-384-2164
Bridgton Academy North Bridgton, ME.	207-647-3322 04057
Brunswick School Greenwich, CT.	203-869-0601 06830

Buckingham Browne & Nichols School Cambridge, MA. 02138	617-864-8668
Canterbury School New Milford, Conn. 06776	203-355-3103 *
Choate Rosemary Hall Wallingford, CT. 06492	203-265-4097 *
Cushing Academy Ashburnham, MA. 01430	617-827-5847
Phillips Exeter Academy Exeter, NH. 03833	603-772-4311 *
Deerfield Academy Deerfield, MA. 01342	413-772-0241 *
Forman School Litchfield, CT. 06759	203-567-4392
Governor Dummer Academy, Blyfield, MA. 01922	508-465-1703
Groton School Groton, MA. 01450	617-448-3367
Gunnery School Washington, CT. 06793	203-868-7334
The Harvey School Katonah, NY 10536	914-232-3161
Hebron Academy Hebron, ME. 04238	207-966-2100
Holderness School Plymouth, NH 03264	603-536-1257
Hotchkiss School Lakeville, CT. 06039	203-435-2591 *
Kent School Kent, CT. 06757	203-927-3501 *

Kents Hill School Kents Hill, ME. 04349	207-685-4914 *
Kimball Union Academy Meriden, NH. 03770	603-469-3211
Kingswood-Oxford School West Hartford, CT. 06119	203-233-9631
Lawrence Academy Groton, MA. 01450	617-448-5635 *
Loomis Chaffee School Windsor, CT. 06095	203-688-4934 *
Marvelwood School Cornwall, CT. 06753	203-672-6612
Middlesex School Concord, MA. 01742	617-369-2550 *
Middlebrook School Millbrook, N.Y. 12545	914-677-8261
Milton Academy Milton, MA. 01286	617-698-7800 *
Moses Brown School Providence, RI 02906	401-831-7350
New Hampton School New Hampton, NH 03256	603-744-8120
New York Military Academy, Cornwall-on-Hudson	914-534-2454
Nichols School Buffalo, NY 4216	716-875-8212 *
Noble and Greenough School, Ded. m, MA. 02026	617-326-3700
Northfield ount Hermon School, Northfield, MA. 01360	413-498-5311
Northwood School Lake Placid, NY 12946	518-523-3357 *

Pingree School South Hamilton, MA. 01982	617-468-4415
Pomfret School Pomfret, CT. 06258	203-928-0671
Portledge School Locust Valley, NY 11560	516-671-1475
Portsmouth Abbey School Portsmouth, RI 02871	401-683-2000
Proctor Academy Andover, N.H. 03216	603-735-5126 *
Providence Country Day School E. Providence, RI 02914	401-438-5170
The Rivers School Weston, MA. 02193	617-235-9300
The Roxbury Latin West Roxbury, MA. 02132	617-325-4920
Salisbury School Salisbury, CT. 06068	203-435-2531
St. George's School Newport, RI 02840	401-847-7565
Saint Mark's School Southborough, MA. 01772	617-485-0050
St. Paul's School Concord, NH 03301	603-225-3341 *
St. Sebastian's Country Day School, Needham, MA. 02192	617-449-5200
South Kent School South Kent, CT. 06785	203-927-3530
Tabor Academy Marion, MA. 02738	617-748-0590
The Taft School Watertown, CT. 06795	203-274-2516 *

Thayer Academy South Braintree, MA. 02184	617-843-3580
Tilton School Tilton, NH 03276	603-286-4342
Trinity-Pawling School Pawling, NY 12564	914-855-3100
Vermont Academy Saxtons River, VT. 05154	802-869-2121 *
Waynflete School Portland, ME. 04102	207-774-5721
Westminster School Simsbury, CT. 06070	203-658-4444 *
Wilbraham & Munson Academy Wilbraham, MA. 01095	413-596-6811
The Williston Northampton School, Easthampton, MA. 01027	413-527-1520
Worcester Academy Worcester, MA. 01604	617-754-5302

LOWER PROFILE NCCA
COLLEGE SPORTS

Golf
Lacrosse
Soccer
Swimming & Diving
Tennis
Outdoor Track & Field and Cross Country
Volleyball
Wrestling

MEN'S GOLF

Division I

Golf is one of the oldest collegiate sports. The first NCAA Competition was held in 1897 with Yale the victor. Golf was mainly an Ivy league game until 1938 when more colleges began to enter the competition.

Golf has two championships. One is a team champion and the second an individual champion. College golf has come a long way in the last 20 years. Many of today's top money earning professionals come form the collegiate ranks. Some former examples of past NCAA individual champions are:

Player	College	NCAA Champion
Jack Nicklaus	Ohio State	1961
Hale Irwin	Colorado	1967
Ben Crenshaw	Texas	1971, 1972, 1973
Tom Kite	Texas	1972
Curtis Strange	Wake Forest	1974

Since golfers take years to mature, more former NCAA graduates are sure to hit the pro circuit.

With collegiate golf there is no winning percentage record. However the top 15 schools based on team standings in 1991 are found below.

Rank	School	Number of Equivalency Scholarships Available	Academic Rank
1	Oklahoma State	5	***
2	Univ. of North Carolina	5	***
3	Arizona State	5	***
4	Wake Forest Univ. (N.C.)	5	****
5	Brigham Young Univ. (Utah)	5	***
6	Georgia Tech.	5	***
7	Southern California	5	***
8	Univ. of Nevada – Las Vegas	5	***
9	University of Arkansas	5	*
10	University of Texas	5	***
11	Univ. of Texas – El Paso	5	**
12	Univ. of Central Florida	5	***
13	Clemson University (S.C.)	5	***
14	North Carolina State Univ.	5	***
15	Univ. of New Mexico	5	**

The top individual champion in 1991 was Warren Schuttle from the University of Nevada at Los Vegas with a 283 score. Phil Mickelson from Arizona State won in 1989 and 1990.

Division II

Division II programs like Division I, offer full golf scholarships to promising student athletes. Because golf requires very few participants the numbers of available scholarships is

low relative to other sports. The Division II calibre is generally one step lower than the Division I level. Very few college
players from Division II have gone on to the professional
ranks. Certainly no big name players, since NCAA Division II
competition began in 1963, have made a name for themselves on the professional circuit.

The host site for the NCAA tournament has been
Florida Atlantic University in 1990 and 1991. The winning
team in both recent years was Florida Southern University.
The top individual champion was Clete Cole from
Columbus with a tournament score of 287.

The top 10 Division II schools based on NCAA 1991
tournament results and their academic reputation are found
below.

1991 Rank	School	Number of Equivalency Scholarships Available	Academic Rank
1	Florida Southern College	4	***
2	Columbus College (GA)	4	**
3	Abilene Christian Univ. (Texas)	4	***
4	Troy St.	4	**
5	Florida Atlantic Univ.	4	***
6	Valdosta State College, GA	4	**
7	Bryant College (Rhode Island)	4	***
8	Jacksonville State Univ. (MS)	4	**
9	Cal St. Stanislaus	4	***
10	Indiana Univ. of Penn.	4	***

Division III

The perennial champion here has been Cal. State at St. Stanislaus. They have won 12 titles. Methodist recently won the team trophy in both 1990 and 1991 under the coaching of Steve Conley. The top 10 schools based on NCAA participation and team scoring in 1991 are listed below. Their academic rating was also considered.

1991 Rank	School	Scholarships	Academic Rank
1	Methodist College (NC)	*	**
2	Gust. Adolphus College		****
3	Ohio Wesleyan Univ.		****
4	Univ. of Cal. at San Diego		****
5	California State at Berdino		***
6	Allegheny College		***
7	Wittenberg Univ. (Ohio)		***
8	Skidmore College (N.Y.)		****
9	Salem State College (Mass.)		**
10	Washington & Lee Univ. (VA)		****

* All Division III sports can only offer financial aid packages not strictly athletic scholarships.

MEN'S LACROSSE

Division I

Lacrosse competition at the Division I level is relatively new. The year 1971 was the first NCAA championship, with Cornell the victor. The national sport of Canada, lacrosse is a game very popular in the northeast United States and Southern Ontario, Canada. Probably the largest factor for why this exciting sport has not gone 'big time' is the lack of a solid, established professional league for players to graduate.

In recent years there have been three schools who are power houses at the NCAA tournament. Syracuse University has won the NCAA Division I trophy four times. Syracuse, in fact, won in 1988, 1989, and 1990. John Hopkins has seven crowns with its last championship back in 1987. North Carolina was the champion in 1991 at the host site of Syracuse University.

The top 10 schools based on NCAA winning percentages at tournament level and academic ranking are found below.

Brendan Cody (No. 14) executes a play for John Hopkins University.
(Courtesy David Preece.)

Rank	School	NCCA Winning %	Number of Equivalency Scholarships	Academic Rank
1	John Hopkins Univ. (MD)	.740	14	*****
2	Syracuse University (N.Y.)	.724	14	****
3	Univ. of North Carolina	.667	14	****
4	Cornell University (N.Y.)	.655	14	*****
5	Univ. of Maryland	.611	14	***
6	Towson State Univ. (MD)	.600	14	***
7	Loyola College (Maryland)	.500	14	***
8	Univ. of Virginia	.483	14	****
9	Navy	.407	14	***
10	Yale	.333	†	*****

† Ivy League schools cannot offer scholarships.

Division III

Like ice hockey, there is no national NCAA competition at Division II. Lacrosse Division III offers good competition but all athletic scholarships are not permitted. Financial assistance packages are what is presented to promising, incoming student athletes. Competition began here in 1980. Hobart College has won every single year.

The top 10 schools based on NCAA tournament winning percentages and academic reputation are found below.

Rank	School	NCCA Winning %	Academic Rank
1	Hobart College (N.Y.)	1.00	****
2	Washington College (MD)	.542	***
3	Ohio Wesleyan Univ.	.500	****
4	Salisbury State University	.438	***
5	Cortland State (N.Y.)	429	***
6	Nazareth College (N.Y.)	.400	***
7	Roanoke College (VA)	.364	***
8	Rochester Inst. of Tech	.333	***
9	Washington & Lee University	.333	****
10	Ithaca College (NY)	.250	***

SOCCER

Men's Division I

Division I soccer generally has a very low profile on college campuses across the U.S. Soccer is, however, developing rapidly at the minor league levels across America. This low cost sport appeals to large numbers of parents. As the interest at the "grass roots" level increases so perhaps will the calibre and presence of college soccer at American schools. Although there is a formal professional soccer league in North America, television revenues for college soccer are practically non-existent. Some players do play pro after leaving collegiate Division I play. UCLA won in 1991.

The top 15 colleges based on NCAA tournament winning percentages in the last 10 years and academic reputation are found below.

Rank	School	NCCA Winning %	Number of Equivalency Scholarships	Academic Rank
1	Univ. of Missouri-St. Louis	.730	11	***
2	Indiana University	.721	11	**
3	Clemson Univ. (S.C.)	.689	11	***
4	Howard Univ. (D.C.)	.654	11	***
5	Univ. of San Francisco	.642	11	***
6	Harvard	.640	11	*****
7	UCLA	.638	11	****
8	Hartwick College (N.Y.)	.615	11	***
9	Loyola (MD) (only 2 years at NCAA tournament)	.667	11	***

10	Southern Illinois Univ. Edwardsville	.613	11	***
11	Duke University (N.C.)	.579	11	*****
12	Univ. of North Carolina	.556	11	****
13	St. Francis College (N.Y.)	.538	11	***
14	Philadelphia College of Textile and Sciences	.528	11	***
15	Univ. of Maryland	.522	11	***

Harvard's Jeremy Amen.
(Photo by Jim Morse.)

Division II

Competition began at the Division II level in 1972 for soccer. Seattle Pacific has won the most championships with four.

The top ten schools based on their NCAA winning percentage (in the last ten years) and academic rank are listed below.

Rank	School	NCCA Winning %	Number of Equivalency Scholarships	Academic Rank
1	Seattle Pacific Univ.	.705	10	***
2	Florida International Univ.	.700	10	***
3	Florida Tech.	.625	10	***
4	Southern Conn. State Univ.	.583	10	***
5	Cal St. Univ. Northridge	.538	10	***
6	Cal St. Univ. Chico	.533	10	***
7	Univ. of Tampa	.526	10	***
8	Univ. of N.C. Greenboro	.500	10	***
9	Oakland Univ. (MI)	.471	10	***
10	Lockhaven Univ. of Penn.	.462	10	***

Division III

Division III soccer is played at a generally competitive level. No scholarships are available here but, of course, we see financial aid packages presented to entice incoming student athletes. The top 10 schools based on NCAA winning percentage (during the last 10 years) and academic reputation are listed below. The 1990 winner was Glassboro State.

Rank	School	NCCA Winning %	Academic Rank
1	Babson College (MA)	.700	****
2	U.C. San Diego	.682	****
3	Glassboro State College (N.J.)	.679	***
4	Washington Univ. (MO)	.654	****
5	Cortland State Univ. (N.Y.)	.636	***
6	Fredonia St. (N.Y.)	.600	***
7	Brandeis Univ. (MA)	.600	****
8	Cal St. San B'dino	.600	***
9	Univ. of Scanton (PA)	.600	***
10	Salem State College (MA)	.600	**

Also note several NESCAC colleges are very competitive but unable to compete at NCAA national tournaments. All NESCAC colleges have a four star or better rating.

MEN'S SWIMMING & DIVING

Division I

Swimming is one of the more traditional NCAA competitions. Competition began in 1925. The first times were kept with non-electronic timing machines. It was not until 1966 that the NCAA adopted electronic timing. The first winner of the 50 yard freestyle was Arthur Rule from Navy at 23.9. In 1991 the champion was Shawn Jordon, Texas at 19.33. Shawn also won the 100 yard freestyle with 42.45. The 200 yard champion was Iowa's Arthur Wojdat at 1.33.71. Team championships began in 1937.

One meter diving began in 1924. The NCAA adopted three meter diving in 1931, and platform diving in 1990.

There are individual national championships for all of the following events;

1. 50 yard freestyle
2. 100 yard freestyle
3. 200 yard freestyle
4. 440 yard freestyle
5. 500 yard freestyle
6. 1,650 yard freestyle
7. 100 yard backstroke
8. 200 yard backstroke
9. 100 yard surface breaststroke
10. 200 yard surface breaststroke
11. 100 yard butterfly breaststroke
12. 200 yard butterfly breaststroke
13. 200 yard individual medley
14. 400 yard individual medley
15. one meter diving
16. three meter diving
17. platform diving
18. 200 yard medley relay
19. 400 yard medley relay

20. 200 yard freestyle relay
21. 400 yard freestyle relay
22. 800 yard freestyle relay

The top ten college *teams* based on team championships in recent years and academic reputation are found below.

Rank	School	Number of Equivalency Scholarships Available	Academic Rank
1	Texas	11	***
2	Stanford	11	*****
3	Southern Cal	11	***
4	Univ. of Tennessee	11	***
5	Univ. of Michigan	11	*****
6	Univ. of Arizona	11	***
7	Southern Methodist	11	***
8	Arizona St.	11	***
9	UCLA	11	****
10	Alabama	11	***

The Division I swimming programs have become excellent training areas for U.S. and Canadian Olympic athletes.

Division II

Scholarships are still presented at the Division II level. These colleges tend to spend less on their pool complex facilities and have much smaller budgets in which to operate. Cal St. Bakersfield has dominated since 1986.

The top ten schools based on 1991 team scoring at the NCAA Championships are below.

Rank	School	Number of Equivalency Scholarships Available	Academic Rank
1	Cal State - Bakersfield	9	***
2	Oakland Univ. (MI)	9	***
3	Clarion Univ. of Penn.	9	***
4	Shippensburg Univ. of Penn.	9	***
5	Univ. of Cal at Davis	9	****
6	Cal St. Chico	9	***
7	State Univ. of NY at Buffalo	9	***
8	Cal Poly SLO	9	***
9	Univ. of North Dakota	9	*
10	Ashland Univ. (Ohio)	9	***

Division III

Division III swimming is a very low profile sport. The budgets are quite small. Team and individual competition began in 1975. The main player here has been Kenyon College coached by Jim Steen. They have won 12 straight national titles.

The top 10 colleges based on 1991 NCAA team scoring and academic reputation are found below.

Rank	School	Scholarships	Academic Rank
1	Kenyon College, Ohio	Financial Aid Packages Only	****
2	Claremount (MS)	"	***
3	Wheaton College (Ill)	Available	****
4	Denison Univ. (Ohio)		***
5	Hope College (MD)		***
6	John Hopkins Univ. (MD)		*****
7	Wabash College (IN)		***
8	Millikin Univ. (Ill)		***
9	Williams College		*****
10	Alleghaeney College (PA)		***

MEN'S TENNIS

Division I

Tennis, once the game of the rich, began very early as an NCAA sport. The first competition was held in 1883. Back then there were two championships, one in the spring and one in the fall. The first few years, Harvard and Yale Colleges bounced the individual championships back and forth. Team competition began in 1946 with Southern Cal the Victor. In 1991, Southern Cal beat Georgia to win.

The top 5 colleges, based on NCAA team championships and academic rankings, are found below.

Rank	School	Number of Equivalency Scholarships	Academic Rank
1	UCLA	15	5	****
2	Southern Cal	13	5	***
3	Stanford	11	5	*****
4	Georgia	2	5	***
5	William and Mary	2	5	***
6	Michigan	2	5	*****
7	Notre Dame	2	5	*****

Division II

Team and singles competition began in 1963. Division II colleges offer limited tennis scholarships because of the small size of the team. The 1991 team NCAA champion was Rollins College coached by Norm Copeland. The runner up was Cal Poly SLO.

The top five colleges for Division II tennis based on NCAA championships in recent years and academic reputations are below.

Rank	School	Number of Equivalency Scholarships	Academic Rank
1	Rollins College (Florida)	5	***
2	Cal Poly SLO	5	***
3	Hampton Univ. (VA)	5	***
4	Chapman College, (CA)	5	***
5	Southern Illinois Univ. Edwardsville	5	***

Division III

Competition at the NCAA Division III tennis level began formally in 1976. Kalamazoo was the first winner and they also won the team crown in 1991. There are no scholarships awarded for Division III tennis. The top five schools based on recent NCAA competition and academic ranking are found below.

Rank	School	Scholarships	Academic Rank
1	Kalamazoo College (MI)	Financial Aid Packages Only	****
2	Swarthmore College (PA)	"	*****
3	Univ. of Cal Santa Cruz		****
4	Washington and Lee Univ. (VA)		****
5	Claremont M-S		

MEN'S OUTDOOR TRACK AND FIELD

Track and field is truly an individual sport that has endured decades of college participation. Team championships began in 1921 when Illinois came in first over Notre Dame at the host site in Chicago. There is a very strong mass appeal for Track and Field. Several television contracts bring in substantial revenues for many conferences. Most athletes at this level are Olympic caliber and many represent their respective countries in international events. There are numerous events for competition. The list is below.

1. 100 metre dash
2. 200 metre dash
3. 400 metre dash
4. 800 metre dash
5. 1,500 metre dash
6. 3,000 metre steeplechase
7. 5,000 metre run
8. 10,000 metre run
9. 110 metre hurdles (all times wind aided)
10. 400 metre hurdles
11. 400 metre relay
12. 1,600 metre relay
13. high jump
14. pole vault
15. long jump
16. triple jump
17. shot put
18. discus throw
19. hammer throw
20. javelin throw
21. decathlon

The team NCAA champion in 1991 was Tennessee coached by Doug Brown. In 1989 and 1990 Louisiana State were national champions.

The top 20 schools based on NCAA team rankings in the 1991 tournament are found below.

Rank	School	Number of Equivalency Scholarships	Academic Rank
1	Univ. of Tennessee	14	****
2	Washington St. Univ. (WA)	14	***
3	Univ. of Oregon	14	***
4	Brigham Young Univ. (Utah)	14	***
5	Univ. of Texas	14	***
6	Louisiana St. Univ.	14	***
7	Univ. of Arkansas	14	***
8	Georgetown Univ. (DC)	14	*****
9	Texas Christian Univ.	14	***
10	Univ. of Georgia	14	***
11	Baylor Univ. (TX)	14	***
12	Texas A & M Univ.	14	***
13	Clemson Univ. (S.C.)	14	***
14	Southern Methodist Univ.	14	***
15	Auburn Univ. (AL)	14	***
16	Univ. of Nebraska	14	***
17	UCLA	14	****
18	George Mason Univ. (VA)	14	***
19	Eastern Michigan Univ.	14	***
20	Univ. of Florida	14	***

The NCAA also holds a championship for Cross Country competition. There are three specific individual champions. One is selected in each; four miles, six miles, and 10,000 metres. There is also a team score. The lowest total point score is the national champion. In 1990 Arkansas with its five member team captured the top award.

The top 15 college programs based on 1990 NCAA competition, academic rankings and interviews with coaches and athletes are found below.

Rank	School	Number of Equivalency Scholarships	Academic Rank
1	Univ. of Arkansas	14	***
2	Iowa St. Univ.	14	***
3	Notre Dame	14	*****
4	Univ. of Texas	14	***
5	Univ. of Oregon	14	***
6	Univ. of Florida	14	***
7	Univ. of Tennessee	14	****
8	Boston U.	14	***
9	Univ. of Wisconsin	14	***
10	Indiana State	14	***
11	Dartmouth College, NH	†	*****
12	Washington	14	***
13	Standford	14	*****
14	Wake forest	14	****
15	Michigan	14	*****

† Ivy League does not permit athletic scholarships.

The number of equivalency scholarships cross country will be reduced to 12.6 per school in 1993-94.

Stanford University's Marc Olesen, now an international cross country competitor and computer executive in California.

VOLLEYBALL

The NCAA brought volleyball to its national table in 1970 - NCAA championships only at one level, Division I. The West Coast colleges have completely dominated this sport. Several players have gone to the Olympic level after graduation in recent years. With the increasing popularity of four-man beach volleyball and the television attention that has begun several ex-collegians are earning top dollars after graduation.

The top five schools who support NCAA volleyball and have competed well in recent years are:

Rank	School	Number of Equivalency Scholarships	Academic Rank
1	UCLA	5	****
2	Southern California	5	***
3	Long Beach St.	5	***
4	Pepperdine	5	****
5	Penn State	5	****

UCLA's Mike Sealy sets the ball.
(Courtesy UCLA.)

MEN'S WRESTLING

Division I

Wrestling is a sport that is very popular at the collegiate level. Of course we are talking about GRECO-ROMAN style, not the completely fake Hollywood, Hulk Hogan variety.

Competition at the Division I level has been around since 1928. The first team winner was Oklahoma State. They also won in 1989 and 1990. Oklahoma State is the huge leader in total team victories. With 29 the next closest school is Iowa with 12 championships followed by Iowa State.

There are individual champions for each of the following weight classes.

- 118 pound
- 126 pound
- 134 pound
- 142 pound
- 150 pound
- 158 pound
- 167 pound
- 177 pound
- 190 pound
- Heavyweight class

Wrestling develops some excellent athletes with super flexibility and strength. Although there are no professional ranks to gravitate to some wrestlers have been known to excel in other sports as well. Carlton Haselrig from the University of Pittsburgh at Johnstown not only won his heavyweight class in Division II but also Division I. He did this four years in a row from 1987-1990. After graduation the Pittsburgh Steelers football team signed him to a contract and are presently developing Carlton into a future starting offensive lineman.

The top five schools at the Division I level based on 1991 NCAA team championship play are found below.

Rank	School	Number of Equivalency Scholarships	Academic Rank
1	Iowa	11	***
2	Oklahoma State	11	***
3	Penn State	11	*****
4	Ohio State	11	*
5	Iowa State	11	***

The top five schools for Division II which also offers wrestling scholarships to promising incoming student athletes are below.

Rank	School	Number of Equivalency Scholarships	Academic Rank
1	Nebraska - Omaha	10	**
2	Central State (OKLA)	10	**
3	Northern Colorado	10	***
4	North Dakota State	10	*
5	Portland State	10	**

Competition at the Division II level began in 1963.

CHAPTER 5

The Academics – A Campus By Campus Analysis

CHOOSING THE RIGHT college — one that will coincide with the goals, interests, talents and personality of each individual — is one of the most important decisions that any young person will ever make. It is also a major investment.

This chapter is an effort to answer questions that students really want to know about academic institutions — questions about academics, financial aid, housing, social life and extracurricular activities.

Each write-up on a college or university includes some basic statistics; address, location, median SAT Scores, percentage of students on financial aid, and the percentages of students who are accepted. Not all schools are covered but rather those which tend to best combine good to excellent learning environments along with good NCAA winning percentages in recent years competing at their division level. Each school has been examined and selected because of its past history in three specific categories: academics, social life and athletic programs. Further information on each campus can be obtained by contacting the school directly. They will be only too pleased to mail a prospective student the campus profile. The schools are my selections as the best match between athletic programs and scholastic environment.

Academics

Is comprised of the overall academic environment of the institution, including its reputation in the academic world, the quality of the faculty, the level of teaching and research, the academic ability of the students, and the quality of facilities.

Social Life / Campus Life

Is primarily a look at the amount of social life that is readily available.

The schools I have selected are my choices for the better campuses providing academics and athletics. These schools have strong traditions of providing young athletes with sound learning environments, both on the field and in the classroom.

The sport each school has completed most successfully in recent years has a sport drawing next to its name.

Key to Symbols

baseball

basketball

cross country

football

golf

hockey

lacrosse

soccer

swim

tennis

track

volleyball

wrestling

AMHERST COLLEGE

- Amherst, Massachusetts
- Admission (413) 542-2328
  Financial Aid (413) 542-2296
- Selective – 21% accepted
- 36% receive financial aid
- SAT scores: 95% score above 500 on verbal;
  96% score above 500 on mathematical

A highly esteemed liberal arts college which devotes itself to undergraduate instruction and faculty members who devote themselves to teaching and research. The campus lies on 100 acres in a small New England town, and an hour and a half drive from Boston.

For a BA, students must take a typical variety of courses but all freshmen must take a two-part course one each semester: Introduction to Liberal Studies. Many major programs prepare students to go directly into technical or professional jobs after graduating. Majors offered include the usual arts and sciences, Asian language, Asian studies, anthropology, astronomy, Black studies, European studies, fine arts, literature, religion, theater and dance.

The varsity sports (Div. III) includes baseball, basketball, crew, cross country, football, golf, hockey, lacrosse, skiing, soccer, squash, swimming track, wrestling.

There are no fraternities. Tuition and fees are in the $15,000 range.

SPORT	CONTACT	TELEPHONE
Hockey	Jack Arena	(413) 542-7950

ARIZONA STATE UNIVERSITY

- Temple Arizona
- Admissions (602) 965-7788
  Financial Aid (602) 965-3355
- 42,000 enrollment
- 60% receive financial aid
- SAT scores: 455 verbal, 529 mathematical

About 73% of applicants are accepted at Arizona. A relatively easy school to enter, Arizona has excellent climate and a host of 11 undergraduate and graduate colleges. Costs are low as in most state schools. Less than $2,000 tuition for in-state and less than $6,000 for out-of-state students.

A small number of students live on campus. It is very much a commuter school.

SPORT	CONTACT	TELEPHONE
Baseball	Jim Brock	(602) 965-3677
Golf	Steve Loy	(602) 965-3262
Swimming	Ron Johnson	(602) 965-2974

UNIVERSITY OF ARIZONA

- Tucson Arizona
- Admissions (602) 621-3237
  Financial Aid (602) 621-1858
- 35,000 enrollment
- SAT scores: 500+ verbal, 500+ mathematical

University of Arizona is a selective school located on over 300 acres in Tucson (500,000 population). Tuition and fees are in the $2,000 range for in-state students and in the $6,000 range for out-of-town pupils.

Sports have a large following both at the varsity and intramural levels. There are 23 fraternities, and 13 sororities on campus.

SPORT	CONTACT	TELEPHONE
Baseball	Jerry Kindall	(602) 621-4102
Swimming	Frank Busch	(602) 621-2131

AUGUSTANA COLLEGE

- Rock Island, Illinois
- Admissions (309) 794-7341
  Financial Aid (309) 794-7207
- 2,100 enrollment
- ACT 24.3 composite, 24.6 mathematical

Augustana College is a liberal arts school located 160 miles west of Chicago. It is very selective with 71% of the incoming students from the top 20% of their high school class. Augustana is famous for its pre-professional preparation. About 70% of all freshmen graduate.

Division III sports are numerous and participation is high. Over 80% of freshmen have started in a varsity sport. Most students live on campus. Tuition and fees run about $9,000.

SPORT	CONTACT	TELEPHONE
Basketball	Steve Yount	(309) 794-7392
Football	Bob Reade	(309) 794-7326

ALLEGHENY COLLEGE

- Meadville, Penn.
- Admissions (814) 332-4351
  Financial Aid (814) 332-4354
- 1,900 enrollment
- SAT scores: 526 verbal, 567 mathematical

Allegheny is a highly selective liberal arts college. It is located about an hour and a half north of Pittsburgh. About 77% of all applicants are accepted. Over 70% of all incoming freshmen graduate. The school has ranked very well nationally in most of its 20 Division III sports. Fraternities and sororities are strong. Tuition and fees are in the $13,000 range.

SPORT	CONTACT	TELEPHONE
Football	Ken O'Keefe	(814) 332-2826
Golf	Norm Sundstrom	(814) 332-2824
Swimming	Tom Erdos	(814) 332-2808

UNIVERSITY OF ALABAMA

- Tuscaloosa, Alabama
- Admissions (205) 348-5666
  Financial Aid (205) 348-6756
- 18,200 enrollment
- SAT scores: 953 combined verbal and mathematical
- 79% of applicants accepted

The University of Alabama is a state supported school located about a one hour drive from Birmingham. The school is located in a city of 73,000 people. It consists of 8 colleges. The percentage of freshmen who eventually graduate is low at 56%. There is strong interest in varsity athletics. About 70% of the students live on or near the campus. There are 28 fraternities and 18 sororities. Tuition is in the $2,200 range in state and $5,000 out of state.

SPORT	CONTACT	TELEPHONE
Football	Gene Stallings	(205) 348-3600

BOSTON UNIVERSITY

- Boston, Massachusetts
- Admission (617) 353-2300
  Financial Aid (617) 353-2965
- 13,000 enrollment
- Very selective – 64% accepted
- 54% receive financial aid
- SAT scores: 77% score above 500 on verbal, 92% score above 500 on mathematical

Boston University is located on the banks of the Charles River. Admission is very selective. Academic pressures vary.

Tuition and fees are in the $15,000 range.

The varsity sports scene (Men Div. I) include baseball, basketball, crew, cross country, football, hockey, sailing, soccer, swimming, tennis, track, and wrestling.

Security is a problem on campus thus peer escort security services are available. The pace is very fast. Freshmen, unmarried and under 21 years of age must live in residence halls. There are 10 fraternities and 9 sororities on campus.

SPORT	CONTACT	TELEPHONE
Hockey	Jack Parker	(617) 353-4639

BOWDOIN COLLEGE

- Brunswick, Maine
- Admissions (207) 725-1000
  Financial Aid (207) 725-3273
- 1,900 enrollment
- Very selective – 24% accepted
- 38% receive financial aid
- SAT scores; 96% score above 500 on verbal, 7% above 700

Bowdoin college has high quality academic offerings. It is located in a small town (pop. 20,000) on 110 acres. Several factors, other than academics are considered in admissions. These are geographical distribution, alumni children, and special talents.

Most students want to go to graduate school after graduation. Majors offered include the usual arts and sciences, Afro-American studies, Arctic studies, Asian studies, chemical physics, and environmental studies/economics.

Varsity sports (Men Div. III) include: Baseball, basketball, cross country, football, golf, hockey, lacrosse, sailing, skiing, squash, soccer, swimming, tennis, track and wrestling.

Tuition and feels are in the $14,000 range.

SPORT	CONTACT	TELEPHONE
Basketball	Tim Gilbride	(207) 725-3352
Hockey	Terry Meagher	(207) 725-3328

BOSTON COLLEGE

- Chestnut Hill, Massachusetts
- Admissions (617) 552-3100
  Financial Aid (617) 552-3320
- 8,700 enrollment
- Very selective – 33% of applicants are accepted
- SAT scores: 67% above 500 on verbal, 83% score above 500 on mathematical

Boston College ranks among the most prestigious Catholic institutions. It is located only minutes from downtown Boston. It has a tradition of preparing a great number of students for training in medicine, law and teaching.

Varsity sports include (Men Div. I): Baseball, basketball, cross country, football, golf, hockey, lacrosse, sailing, skiing, soccer, swimming, tennis, track and wrestling.

More than half of the students at Boston college live on campus. Tuition and fees are in the $14,000 range. There are no fraternities or sororities.

SPORT	CONTACT	TELEPHONE
Cross Country	Karen Keith	(617) 552-3008
Hockey	Len Ceglarski	(617) 552-3028

BABSON COLLEGE

- Wellesley, Massachusetts
- Admissions (617) 239-552
  Financial Aid (617) 239-4001
- 1,500 enrollment
- 35% receive financial aid
- SAT scores: average scores 500 on verbal, 590 on mathematical

Babson college is located in a Boston suburb, Wellesley (pop. 30,000). Careers in business and industry are pursued by more than 90% of graduates who attend Babson.

Varsity sports (mens Div. III) include: Baseball, basketball, cross country, golf, hockey (II), squash, soccer, swimming, tennis, lacrosse, and skiing.

There are four fraternities, and two sororities. Tuition and fees are in the $15,000 range.

SPORT	CONTACT	TELEPHONE
Hockey	Steve Stirling	(617) 239-4250
Soccer	Jon Anderson	(617) 239-4250

BEMIDJI STATE UNIVERSITY

- Bemidji, Minn.
- Admissions (218) 755-2040
  Financial Aid (218) 755-2034
- 4,000 enrollment
- ACTscores: 19.3 composite, 17.9 mathematical
- 85% receive financial aid

Bemidji State is a state supported school where most graduates of the top 50% of their high school class are accepted. About 77% of all applicants are accepted. Most sports are at the Division II level. Hockey has competed well at Division III. The majority of students commute to campus. Tuition and fees are in the $2,000 range in-state and $4,500 for out-of-state.

SPORT	CONTACT	TELEPHONE
Hockey	Bob Peters	(218) 755-2769

BRIGHAM YOUNG UNIVERSITY

- Provo, Utah
- Admissions (801) 378-2507
  Financial Aid (801) 378-4104
- 28,000 enrollment
- ACTscores: 25.2 composite, 25.3 mathematical
- 77% receive financial aid

Brigham Young is a Mormon based school. It is a selective university where about 80% of all applicants are accepted. About 65% of all freshmen graduate. Seven classes in religion are required for graduation. The principals of the Mormon faith are in force.

Tuition and fees run in the $2,000 for those of the Mormon faith. Non-Mormons pay in the $3,200 range.

SPORT	CONTACT	TELEPHONE
Football	LaVell Edwards	(801) 378-2916
Golf	Karl Tucker	(801) 378-7304
Track	Willard Hirschi	(801) 378-3329

BROWN UNIVERSITY

- Providence, Rhode Island
- Admissions (401) 863-2378
  Financial Aid (401) 863-2721
- 3,500 enrollment
- Very selective – 20% of applicants are accepted
- 53% receive financial aid
- SAT scores: 607 verbal, 669 mathematical

One of the oldest, and most selective universities in the country, Brown places its emphasis on undergraduate instruction. It is located in the residential town of Providence on 40 acres of land.

Majors offered include the usual arts and sciences as well as applied mathematics, Asian studies, chemistry, engineering, international relations, linguistics, and public policy.

Varsity sports include (Men Div. I): Baseball, basketball, crew, cross country, football, ice hockey, lacrosse, soccer, swimming / diving, tennis, track, water polo and wrestling.

Students attending Brown are very concerned with academics. There are ten fraternities and two sororities on campus, and freshmen are given preference in college housing if all students cannot be accommodated. Tuition and fees are in the $16,000 range.

SPORT	CONTACT	TELEPHONE
Hockey	Bob Gaudet	(401) 863-2802

CALIFORNIA STATE POLYTECHNIC UNIVERSITY / PONOMA

- Ponoma, CA
- Admissions (714) 869-2000
  Financial Aid (714) 869-3700
- 19,000 total enrollment
- 25% receive financial aid
- SAT scores: 408 verbal, 532 mathematical

Cal Poly/Ponoma is located on 1,400 acres in a city of 104,000 just half an hour from Los Angeles. 63% of all applicants are accepted. Tuition for in-state students is in the $1,000 range and for out-of-state students $7,000.

SPORT	CONTACT	TELEPHONE
Baseball	John Scolinos	(714) 869-2774

CALIFORNIA STATE - FULLERTON

- Fullerton, CA
- Admissions (714) 773-2370
  Financial Aid (714) 773-3125
- 17,000 enrollment
- 25% receive financial aid
- SAT scores: 414 verbal, 476 mathematical

SCU Fullerton is largely a commuter school. Over 80% of all students travel over five miles to class. Off campus housing was increased rapidly in recent years. There are no university residential facilities. Tuition is in the $1,000 range for in-state applicants and $7,000 for those out-of-state.

SPORT	CONTACT	TELEPHONE
Baseball	Augie Garrido	(714) 773-3789

UCLA

- Los Angeles, California
- Admissions (310) 825-3101
  Financial Aid (310) 206-0400
- 11,000 male, 11,800 female
- 34,000 total enrollment
- SAT scores: 528 verbal, 627 mathematical
- Very selective
- 43% receive financial aid

This campus is the largest of the University of California. UCLA is an excellent school with only 41% of the applicants being accepted.

A huge variety of courses and majors are to be found. All of the faculty hold PhD or equivalent. The school does not actively seek a national student body.

Campus life is quite easy going and a high percentage of students live off campus. Student interest in intramural and varsity athletics is quite high. The presence of fraternities and sororities is also large. Parking is a problem on campus.

Tuition is inexpensive (about $2,000) for in-state applicants and $8,000 for out-of-state. UCLA is a bargain.

SPORT	CONTACT	TELEPHONE
Basketball	Jim Harrick	(310) 825-8699
Football	Terry Donahue	(310) 825-8699
Soccer	Sigi Schmid	(310) 825-8699
Swimming	Ron Ballatore	(310) 825-8699
Tennis	Glen Bassett	(310) 825-8699
Track	Bob Larsen	(310) 825-8699
Volleyball	Al Scates	(310) 825-8699

CHAPMAN COLLEGE

- Orange, CA
- Admissions (714) 997-6711
  Financial Aid (714) 997-6741
- 2,100 enrollment
- SAT scores: 451 verbal, 490 mathematical
- 75% receive financial aid

Chapman is a private liberal arts school located 32 miles southeast of Los Angeles. A conservative school where all undergraduates under 21 are required to live in college dormitories. Tuition and fees are in the $13,000 range.

SPORT	CONTACT	TELEPHONE
Baseball	Mike Weathers	(714) 997-6691
Tennis	Reddy Gustine	(714) 997-6691

CALIFORNIA POLYTECHNIC STATE UNIVERSITY/ SAN LOUIS OBISPO

- San Luis Obispo, CA
- Admissions (805) 756-2311
  Financial Aid (805) 756-2927
- SAT scores: 463 verbal, 565 mathematical
- 40% receive financial aid

Cal Poly / SLO is a coastal campus of 5,160 acres. It is found right in the middle of San Francisco and Los Angeles. Only about 30% of the applicants are accepted. It is a selective school. About half of all incoming students graduate. Over 80% of the students live in off-campus housing. Varsity sports are numerous and have a good following. Tuition and fees are low at around $1,200 in-state and $5,000 for out-of-state, making this school of good value for the money.

SPORT	CONTACT	TELEPHONE
Football	Lyle Setencich	(805) 756-2650
Swimming	Rich Firman	(805) 756-2650
Tennis	Kevin Platt	(805) 756-2777

CSU - ST. STANISLAUS

- Turlock, CA
- Admissions (209) 667-3151
  Financial Aid (209) 667-3336
- 3,900 enrollment
- SAT scores: 388 verbal, 463 mathematical
- 79% of applicants accepted

The campus is a 230 acre area located in a town of 24,000. A selective school where 80% of the faculty have PhD's. Tuition is in the $1,000 area for in-state and $8,000 for out-of-state.

SPORT	CONTACT	TELEPHONE
Baseball	Jim Bowen	(209) 667-3328

UC - RIVERSIDE

- Riverside, CA
- Admissions (714) 787-3411
  Financial Aid (714) 787-3878
- 6,500 enrollment
- SAT scores: 467 verbal, 560 mathematical
- 74% of applicants accepted

The school was founded in 1954. It is located about 50 miles east of Los Angeles. UC - Riverside is a high quality school with intense academic pressures. Tuition for in-state students is in the $2,500 range and in the $8,000 range for out-of-state students.

SPORT	CONTACT	TELEPHONE
Baseball	Jim Smitheran	(714) 787-5441
Basketball	John Masi	(714) 787-4124

COLGATE UNIVERSITY

- Hamilton, New York
- Admissions (315) 824-1000
  Financial Aid (315) 824-1000
- 2,600 enrollment
- Highly selective
- 46% receive financial aid
- SAT scores: 604 verbal, 667 mathematical

The university is located in a small town 40 miles from Syracuse. Competition at the school is very intense and academics are a number one concern. Many graduates leave with a degree in business or teaching.

Varsity sports include (Men Div. I): Baseball, basketball, cross country, football, golf, hockey, lacrosse, soccer, swimming, tennis, and track. Hockey and football are the most popular intercollegiate sports, drawing great crowds for both. Tuition and fees are in the $16,000 range.

There are 10 fraternities and 5 sororities on campus and freshmen are required to live in residence halls.

SPORT	CONTACT	TELEPHONE
Hockey	Don Vaughan	(315) 824-7583

CORNELL UNIVERSITY

- Ithaca, New York
- Admissions (607) 256-5421
  Financial Aid (607) 256-5145
- 13,000 enrollment
- Most selective – 29% applicants accepted
- 45% receive financial aid
- SAT scores; 594 verbal, 685 mathematical

Cornell University is a private school and a member of the

Ivy League. It lies on 740 acres in central New York.

Varsity sports include (Men Div. I): Baseball, basketball, crew, cross country, fencing, football, golf, gymnastics, hockey, lacrosse, shooting, skiing, soccer squash, swimming, tennis, track, wrestling.

Approximately 53% live in off-campus housing. There are 47 fraternities and 16 sororities on campus. Tuition and fees are in the $16,000 range.

SPORT	CONTACT	TELEPHONE
Hockey	Brian McCutcheon	(607) 255-4171
Lacrosse	Richie Moran	(607) 225-7332

COLBY COLLEGE

- Waterville, Maine
- Admissions (207) 872-3168
  Financial Aid (207) 872-3379
- 1,700 enrollment
- Highly selective – 44% applicants accepted
- 33% receive financial aid
- SAT scores: 550 verbal, 600 mathematical

The university is typically New England located on the outskirts of a small community. It is a school for those who love the outdoors.

Varsity sports include (Men Div. III): Baseball, basketball, cross country, football, golf, ice hockey, lacrosse, soccer, squash, swimming, tennis track.

Tuition and fees are in the $15,000 range.

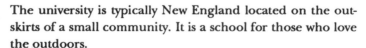

SPORT	CONTACT	TELEPHONE
Hockey	Charlie Corey	(207) 872-3368

UNIVERSITY OF DENVER

- Denver, Colorado
- Admissions (303) 871-2036
  Financial Aid (303) 871-2681
- 6,800 enrollment
- Selective – 73% of applicants accepted
- 60% receive financial aid

The University of Denver is located about 5 minutes from downtown Denver. Admission is selective and applicants must apply by March 15.

Varsity sports include baseball, basketball (I), hockey (III), lacrosse, soccer, swimming, tennis.

Approximately 70% of men live in coed dorms. There are 9 fraternities and 6 sororities on campus. Tuition and fees are in the $13,000 range.

SPORT	CONTACT	TELEPHONE
Hockey	Frank Serratore	(303) 871-3397

DUKE UNIVERSITY

- Durham, N.C.
- Admissions (919) 684-3214
  Financial Aid (919) 684-6225
- 10,300 enrollment
- SAT scores: 612 verbal, 694 mathematical
- 26% of all applicants accepted

Duke is a big name institution. It is located in a city of 100,000 about 250 miles southwest of Washington, D.C. Duke is one of the hardest schools to enter academically in North America. High ability students are the norm at Duke.

Tuition is in the $15,000 range.

SPORT	CONTACT	TELEPHONE
Basketball	Mike Krzyzewski	(919) 684-3777
Soccer	John Rennie	(919) 684-2120

ELMIRA COLLEGE

- Elmira, New York
- 1,900 enrollment
- SAT scores: 460 verbal, 480 mathematical
- 80% receive financial aid

Elmira is a liberal arts college on 38 acres, located in a city of 35,000. It is about an hour and a half drive west of Syracuse. About 74% of all applicants are accepted. One quarter of its freshmen class leave after year one. Most students live on or near campus. Tuition and fees run about $10,000.

SPORT	CONTACT	TELEPHONE
Hockey	Glenn Thomaris	(607) 739-8787

FLORIDA SOUTHERN COLLEGE

- Lakeland, Florida
- Admissions (813) 680-4140
- 1,700 enrollment
- SAT scores: 450 verbal, 500 mathematical
- 82% receive financial aid

Florida Southern is located 35 miles east of Tampa. It is a church related school with six semester hours of religion required for all students. No alcohol is allowed. Tuition is in the $7,000 area.

SPORT	CONTACT	TELEPHONE
Baseball	Chuck Anderson	(813) 680-4266
Golf	Charley Matlock	(813) 680-4261

FURMAN UNIVERSITY

- Greenville, South Carolina
- Admissions (803) 294-2034
  Financial Aid (803) 294-3128
- 2,800 enrollment
- SAT scores: 544 verbal, 620 mathematical
- 70% receive financial aid

Furman is a very selective school of a southern baptist flavor. It is located on a 750 acre campus near Greenville which has a population of 62,000. About 86% of all freshmen have graduated in the top 20% of their high school class. Only about half of all applicants are accepted. Almost 100% of the faculty hold a PhD or equivalent. Alcohol is not permitted on campus. There is a large following in the varsity sports. Tuition and fees are about $9,000.

SPORT	CONTACT	TELEPHONE
Football	Jimmy Sutterfield	(803) 294-2120

GEORGETOWN UNIVERSITY

- Washington, D.C.
- Admissions (202) 687-3600
  Financial Aid (202) 687-4547
- 11,600 students
- SAT scores: 628 verbal, 683 mathematical
- 22% of applicants accepted

Georgetown University is a Roman Catholic school. All undergraduate students must fulfill requirements in theology and philosophy. It is located on a 110 acre campus 10 minutes from downtown Washington. Admission is among the most selective in North America. Tuition is in the $13,000 range. Interest in varsity sports is very high. About 80% of the students live in co-ed dormitories.

SPORT	CONTACT	TELEPHONE
Basketball	John Thompson, Jr.	(703) 687-2374
Track	Frank Gagliano	(703) 687-2445

GEORGIA SOUTHERN COLLEGE

- Statesboro, GA
- Admissions (912) 681-5531
  Financial Aid (912) 681-5413
- 9,900 enrollment
- SAT scores: 444 verbal, 482 mathematical
- 45% receive financial aid

Georgia Southern is a state supported school located about one hour west of Savannah, a town of 18,000 people. About 88% of all applicants are accepted. Over one third of all freshmen do not return for the sophomore year.

About 70% of the students live on campus. Varsity sports are of a significant interest to most. Tuition and fees are approximately $2,000 in-state and $4,500 for out-of-state applicants.

SPORT	CONTACT	TELEPHONE
Football	Tim Stowers	(912) 681-5522

UNIVERSITY OF GEORGIA

- Athens, Georgia
- Admissions (404) 542-2112
  Financial Aid (404) 542-6147
- 26,000 enrollment
- SAT scores: 496 verbal, 560 mathematical
- 50% of students receive financial aid

University of Georgia is a 1,500 acre campus with 13 schools and colleges. It is located 65 miles east of Atlanta. University of Georgia is a selective school with about 74% of applicants being accepted.

Interest in varsity and intramural athletics is very high.

SPORT	CONTACT	TELEPHONE
Baseball	Steve Webber	(404) 542-7915
Tennis	Manuel Diaz	(404) 542-1622
Track	John Mitchell	(404) 542-7915

HAMILTON COLLEGE

- Clinton, New York
- Admissions (315) 859-4421
  Financial Aid (315) 859-4434
- Highly selective – 42% applicants accepted
- 70% receive financial aid
- SAT scores: 559 verbal, 609 mathematical

Hamilton College is a high quality, coed college. The campus is located on 350 acres one mile from Clinton (pop. 2,400). Admission is very selective. Hamilton is an excellent feeder for Ivy League Graduate programs. The academic pressures are intense. Many alumni assist in both career guidance and job placement. The New York Times magazine rated Hamilton as one of the top ten small colleges in the country.

After graduating about 17% of the students enter graduate school.

The college has above average facilities, and interest in intramural and intercollegiate athletics is very high. Students have a great deal of control over social life on campus.

Tuition and fees are in the $16,000 range.

SPORT	CONTACT	TELEPHONE
Basketball	Tom Murphy	(315) 859-4114
Hockey	Phil Grady	(315) 859-4114
Swimming	Dave Thompson	(315) 859-4114

HARVARD UNIVERSITY

- Cambridge, Massachusetts
- Admissions (617) 495-1551
- 16,871 total graduate and undergraduate
- Highly selective – 17% of applicants accepted
- 58% receive financial aid
- SAT scores: 500-800

The main campus is located across the Charles River from Boston in Cambridge, a city of 100,800. Harvard's admission standards are among the most selective in the country. The facilities are excellent. The university's library is the largest university library in the world.

A very high percentage of faculty members hold doctorate degrees, making Harvard one of the best in the country.

Varsity sports include (Men Div. I): Baseball, basketball, crew, fencing, football, golf, ice hockey, lacrosse, sailing, skiing, squash, soccer, swimming, tennis, track, volleyball, water polo, and wrestling.

SPORT	CONTACT	TELEPHONE
Hockey	Ronn Tomassoni	(617) 495-2418
Soccer	Michael Getman	(617) 495-4549

THE JOHN HOPKINS UNIVERSITY

- Baltimore, Maryland
- Admissions (301) 516-8171
  Financial Aid (301) 516-8028
- 13,000 enrollment
- SAT scores: 599 verbal, 699 mathematical
- 58% receive financial aid

John Hopkins is located on 140 acres in a residential area near Baltimore. The school is among the most selective in the United States. Only 43% of all applicants are accepted. Almost 90% of incoming freshmen are graduates from the top 20% of their high school class. Academic pressures are strong. About 87% of all freshmen graduate. There is a strong interest in intramural sports. Lacrosse is the big sport on campus.

Tuition and fees are in the $15,000 range.

SPORT	CONTACT	TELEPHONE
Lacrosse	Tony Seaman	(410) 338-7479
Swimming	George Kennedy	(410) 338-7484

HOBART AND SMITH COLLEGES

- Geneva, New York
- Admissions (315) 789-5500
  Financial Aid (315) 789-5500
- 2,000 enrollment
- SAT scores: 523 verbal, 590 mathematical

Hobart is a private, liberal arts school which shares facilities with William Smith College. Admission is very selective. Only 47% of all applicants are accepted. Division III sports dominate, but Division I lacrosse does very well. Most students live on campus. Tuition and fees are in the $14,000 range.

SPORT	CONTACT	TELEPHONE
Lacrosse	BJ O'Hara	(315) 781-3564

ITHACA COLLEGE

- Ithaca, NY
- (607)274-3124;
  Financial Aid (607)274-3131
- 5,800 enrollment
- SAT 514 Verbal, 556 Math

Ithaca is a small liberal arts college located about a 45 minute drive south of Syracuse. It is a 400 acre campus. Almost 60% of all applicants are accepted. Most students live on campus. Division III sports are numerous and football is the big attraction. Tuition and fees are about $12,000.

SPORT	CONTACT	TELEPHONE
Football	Jim Butterfield	(607) 274-3748
Lacrosse	Jeff Long	(607) 274-3747

KENTUCKY WESLEYAN COLLEGE

- Owensboro, Ky
- Admissions (502) 926-3111
  Financial Aid (502) 926-3111
- 800 enrollment
- ACT 21, 85% of applicants from 2/5's of
  high school graduating class

This school is a church-related college in a city of 60,000. It was founded in 1858. About 67% of all applicants are accepted. Two courses in religion are required of all students. Most students live on campus. Tuition and fees are in the $6,000 range.

SPORT	CONTACT	TELEPHONE
Basketball	Wayne Boultinghouse	(502) 683-4795

LE MOYNE COLLEGE

- Syracuse, NY
- Admissions (315)445-4300
  Financial Aid (315) 445-4400
- 2,000 enrollment
- SAT scores: 518 verbal, 560 mathematical
- 80% receive financial aid

Le Moyne college is located on a 140 acre campus. It is a Roman Catholic based school. Tuition and fees are around $9,000. About 67% of applicants are accepted.

SPORT	CONTACT	TELEPHONE
Baseball	Richard Rockwell	(315) 445-4450

MARIETTA COLLEGE

- Marietta, Ohio
- Admissions (614) 374-4600
  Financial Aid (614) 374-4714
- 1,300 enrollment
- SAT scores: 460 verbal, 515 mathematical
- 65% receive financial aid

Marietta is a liberal arts college located on a 60 acre campus about one hour southeast of Columbus, Ohio.

About 77% of applicants are accepted.

Most students live on campus.

SPORT	CONTACT	TELEPHONE
Baseball	Don Schaly	(614) 374-4673

UNIVERSITY OF MAINE

- Orono, ME
- Admissions (207) 581-1561
  Financial Aid (207) 581-1324
- 12,200 total enrollment
- 88% accepted
- 50% receive financial aid
- SAT scores: 470 verbal, 520 mathematical

The University of Maine has seven undergraduate colleges on the campus: engineering (one of the best) and science, education, life science and agriculture, arts and sciences, forest resources, business administration and Bangor Community College (a two year technical school).

The University offers 123 athletic scholarships each year. Football, baseball and ice hockey are the most prominent and popular sports.

Students also enjoy skiing at Sugarloaf mountain and

swimming at the beaches near Bar Harbor. Tuition and fees are in the $2,500 range for in-state and $6,000 for out-of-state applicants.

SPORT	CONTACT	TELEPHONE
Hockey	Shawn Walsh	(207) 581-1106

UNIVERSITY OF MICHIGAN

- Ann Arbor, Michigan
- Admissions (313) 764-7433
  Financial Aid (313) 763-6600
- 35,800 enrollment
- 56% accepted
- 50% receive financial aid
- SAT scores: 560 verbal, 630 mathematical

The University of Michigan is considered to be one of the top ten in the country and provides an excellent undergraduate liberal arts education, the best being the social sciences. There is a great deal of competition at the University of Michigan, and studying is a first priority.

There are 336 partial athletic scholarships available for men and women. No matter what the social activity, football overshadows all else.

Freshmen are guaranteed housing and can specify their first three dorm choices and desired number of roommates. Tuition and fees are in the $4,500 range for in-state and $13,000 for out-of-state students.

SPORT	CONTACT	TELEPHONE
Baseball	Jim Freehan	(313) 747-2583
Basketball	Steve Fisher	(313) 763-5504
Cross Country	Ron Warhurst	(313) 747-2583
Football	Gary Moeller	(313) 747-2583
Hockey	Red Berenson	(313) 747-2583
Tennis	Brian Eisner	(313) 747-2583
Swimming	Jon Urbanek	(313) 747-2583

MICHIGAN STATE UNIVERSITY
- East Lansing, Michigan
- Admissions (517) 355-8332
  Financial Aid (517) 353-5940
- 45,000 enrollment
- 50% accepted
- 60% receive financial aid
- SAT scores: 460 verbal, 520 mathematical

One of the nation's largest schools, Michigan state has a great variety of undergraduate majors from business to agriculture to hotel and restaurant management to the sciences.

Athletic and honors students get first crack at undergraduate courses — a big plus because some courses are very difficult to get into. MSU has had many national champion sports. Tuition and fees are in the $3,500 range in-state and $9,000 for out-of-state students.

SPORT	CONTACT	TELEPHONE
Basketball	Jud Heathcote	(517) 355-1643
Hockey	Ron Mason	(517) 355-1639

MIDDLEBURY COLLEGE

- Middlebury, Vermont
- Admissions (802) 388-3711
  Financial Aid (802) 388-3711
- 1,900 enrollment
- Very selective, 38% accepted
- 65% receive financial aid
- SAT scores: 600 verbal, 650 mathematical

Middlebury College, located about 120 miles from Montreal on a 250-acre campus.

Varsity sports (Men Div. III) include basketball, cross country, football, hockey (II), lacrosse, alpine and Nordic skiing (I), soccer, squash, swimming, tennis, track.

There is strong interest in fraternities and sororities and students are active in winter recreational activities. Tuition and fees are in the $20,000 range.

SPORT	CONTACT	TELEPHONE
Hockey	Bill Beaney	(802) 388-3711

MICHIGAN TECHNOLOGICAL UNIVERSITY

- Houghton, Michigan
- Admissions (906) 487-2335
  Financial Aid (906) 487-2622
- 6,500 enrollment
- SAT scores: 494 verbal, 619 mathematical
- 68% receive financial aid

Michigan Tech is a state supported school located 420 miles north of Chicago. It is a very selective school where over 70 % of its freshmen class graduated in the top 20% of their high school class. About 83% of all applicants are accepted.

About 70% of the students live on or near the campus. Hockey is the only Division I sport and has a large following. Tuition and fees run about $3,000 in-state and $6,000 for out-of-state.

SPORT	CONTACT	TELEPHONE
Hockey	Newell Brown	(906) 487-3070

CENTRAL MICHIGAN UNIVERSITY

- Mount Pleasant, Michigan
- Admissions (517) 774-3076
  Financial Aid (517) 774-3674
- ACT scores: 20.7 composite, 20.6 mathematical
- 70% receive financial aid

Central Michigan is a state funded school in a town of 25,000 people. It is located about a one hour drive from Lansing. About 70% of all applicants are accepted. About 22% of the students commute to classes. Sports are of a major interest on campus. The campus has 14 fraternities and 14 sororities. Tuition and fees are in the $2,200 range and $5,000 for out-of-state.

SPORT	CONTACT	TELEPHONE
Football	Herb Deromedi	(517) 774-6667

UNIVERSITY OF MINNESOTA – TWIN CITIES

- Minneapolis, Minnesota
- 46,440 total enrollment
- 78% applicants accepted
- 42% receive financial aid
- SAT scores: 490 verbal, 560 mathematical

One of the largest campuses in the nation, the University of Minnesota offers more than 250 majors. The academic facilities are excellent, but class size can be as many as 950 and often undergraduates have difficulty getting the courses they want. Most students live off-campus. Athletics are very popular at the University of Minnesota with excellent hockey and basketball teams. Tuition and fees are in the $3,000 range in-state and $7,000 for out-of-state.

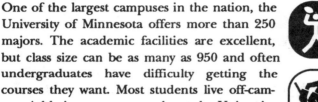

SPORT	CONTACT	TELEPHONE
Baseball	John Anderson	(612) 625-1060
Basketball	Clem Haskins	(612) 625-3085
Football	John Gutekunst	(612) 624-6004
Hockey	Doug Woog	(612) 625-0015

UNIVERSITY OF NEBRASKA-LINCOLN

- Lincoln, Nebraska
- Admissions (402) 472-2023
  Financial Aid (402) 472-2030
- 24,000 enrollment
- ACT scores: 22.7 composite,
  22.6 mathematical
- 58% receive financial aid

The University of Nebraska is located in Lincoln, a city of 172,000 people. The school is selective in admission but nearly 94% of all applicants are accepted. Only about one half of incoming freshmen eventually graduate. A high 30% of first year students do not return for year two. All freshmen must live on campus. Fraternities and varsity sports dominate. Tuition and fees are in the $2,200 range and $5,000 for out-of-state students.

SPORT	CONTACT	TELEPHONE
Football	Tom Osborne	(402) 472-3116
Track	Gary Pepin	(402) 472-6461

UNIVERSITY OF NEVADA

- Las Vegas, Nevada
- Admissions (702) 739-3443
  Financial Aid (702) 739-3424
- 15,000 enrollment
- ACT scores: 17.1 composite,
  18.7 mathematics
- easily accepted

The University of Las Vegas is a state school on a 300 acre campus. A surprising 42% of freshmen do not return for their second year. Tuition for in-state students is in the $2,000 range and out-of-state students pay $6,000.

SPORT	CONTACT	TELEPHONE
Basketball	Jerry Tarkanian	(702) 739-3295
Golf	Dwaine Knight	(702) 739-3714

UNIVERSITY OF NORTH CAROLINA
AT CHAPEL HILL

- Chapel Hill, North Carolina
- Admissions (919) 966-3621
  Financial Aid (919) 962-8396
- 23,600 enrollment
- SAT scores: 1101 combined scores
- 31% of applicants accepted

Chapel Hill was the United States' first state
university founded in 1789. The University of
North Carolina has 14 schools and colleges on a
500 acre campus. The school is located a half
hour from Raleigh. Tuition and fees for in-state
students are very low at the 1,500 range. Out-of-
state students pay in the $6,000 range, making
the University of North Carolina a steal.

SPORT	CONTACT	TELEPHONE
Basketball	Dean Smith	(919) 962-1155
Golf	Devon Brouse	(919) 962-2349
Lacrosse	Dave Klarmann	(919) 962-6000
Soccer	Anson Dorrance	(919) 962-5411

NORTH CAROLINA STATE UNIVERSITY

- Raleigh, North Carolina
- Admissions (919) 737-2437
  Financial Aid (919) 737-2421
- 25,600 enrollment
- SAT scores: 494 verbal, 582 mathematics
- 63% of applicants are accepted

North Carolina State is a major technological university. It has a 30% engineering student enrollment. North

Carolina is very selective and a bargain because of its inexpensive state school prices. Tuition and fees are in the $1,500 range and in the $6,000 range for out-of-state students

SPORT	CONTACT	TELEPHONE
Basketball	Les Robinson	(919) 737-2104
Golf	Richard Sykes	(919) 737-2053

UNIVERSITY OF NOTRE DAME
- Notre Dame, Indiana
- Admissions (219) 239-7505
  Financial Aid (219) 239-6436
- 9,900 enrollment
- SAT scores: 567 verbal, 652 mathematics
- 67% receive financial aid

Notre Dame is a Roman Catholic sponsored school of national distinction. It is highly selective in admission. Notre Dame only became co-ed in 1972. The 1,250 acre campus is located north of South Bend, Indiana (population 126,000) and an hour and a half east of Chicago. About 34% of all applicants are accepted. Only 2% of freshmen do not return for the second year of college. On average, all freshmen (92%) graduate within four years.

Each student must take courses in theology. Of course football is the major interest on campus. No alcohol is allowed on campus grounds. Most students live on campus. Tuition and fees are in the $12,000 range.

SPORT	CONTACT	TELEPHONE
Cross Country	Joe Piane	(219) 239-6135
Football	Lou Holtz	(219) 239-7475
Tennis	Bobby Bayliss	(219) 239-6107

NORTH PARK COLLEGE

- Chicago, Illinois
- Admissions (312) 583-2700
  Financial Aid (312) 583-2700
- 1,000 enrollment
- SAT scores: 530 verbal, 456 mathematics

North Park is a liberal arts college where about 63% of applicants are accepted. Tuition and fees are in the $9,000 range. About 75% of the student body receive financial aid. Downtown Chicago is only 20 minutes away. Alcohol is not allowed on campus.

SPORT	CONTACT	TELEPHONE
Basketball	Bosko Djurickovic	(312) 583-2700

OKLAHOMA STATE UNIVERSITY

- Stillwater, Oklahoma
- Admissions (405) 744-6857
  Financial Aid (405) 744-6604
- 16,000 enrollment
- B average in high school, 19 ACT composite
- 88% of applicants accepted
- 47% receive financial aid

Oklahoma State is an old established 415 acre campus. It is located an hour drive northeast of Oklahoma City.

Varsity sports are big on campus. Alcohol is not allowed on campus or in fraternity or sorority houses. Tuition and fees are in the $2,000 range and in the $5,000 range for out-of-state students.

SPORT	CONTACT	TELEPHONE
Basketball	Eddie Sutton	(405) 744-5845
Football	Pat Jones	(405) 744-5737
Golf	Mike Holder	(405) 744-7259
Wrestling	Joe Seay	(405) 744-5854

PENNSYLVANIA STATE UNIVERSITY (PENN STATE)

- University Park, Pennsylvania
- Admissions (215) 898-7507
  Financial Aid (215) 898-7996
- 38,000 enrollment
- SAT scores: 518 verbal, 614 mathematics
- 73% receive financial aid

Penn State began in 1855 and is located on 290 acres. It is a huge school which has 17 commonwealth campuses and a large 4,200 acre agricultural experiment area. Admission is difficult, with only 34% of all applicants being accepted. There are strong schools of engineering and mineral sciences.

About 60% of all incoming freshmen graduate eventually. Penn State has a large range of intramural sports. Drinking is prohibited on campus. About 55% of the students live in off-campus housing. Tuition and fees are in the $4,500 range and in the $9,000 range for those students who are out-of-state.

SPORT	CONTACT	TELEPHONE
Football	Joe Paterno	(814) 865-0411
Volleyball	Tom Peterson	(814) 863-7464
Wrestling	Rick Lorenzo	(814) 865-9631

PRINCETON UNIVERSITY

- Princeton, New Jersey
- 4,400 enrollment
- Very selective, 16% applicants accepted
- 43% receive financial aid
- SAT scores: 624 verbal, 674 mathematics

A member of the Ivy League, Princeton University, located on a 2,600 acre campus about an hour from New York City, is one of the best schools in the country.

Varsity sports include (Men Div. I) baseball, basketball, crew, cross country, fencing, football, golf, hockey, lacrosse, soccer, squash, swimming/diving, tennis, track, volleyball, water polo, wrestling. There are no fraternities or sororities. Tuition and fees are in the $14,000 range.

SPORT	CONTACT	TELEPHONE
Hockey	Don Cahoon	(609) 258-5058

ROCHESTER INSTITUTE OF TECHNOLOGY

- Rochester, New York
- Admissions (716) 475-6631
  Financial Aid (716) 475-2186
- 13,100 enrollment
- Selective, 83% applicants accepted
- 64% receive financial aid
- SAT scores: 483 verbal, 579 mathematics

Located on a 1,300 acre campus, Rochester Institute of Technology offers a number of special courses; printing, photography, and photographic science. Co-op courses are also available after sophomore year in business, science, and engineering.

Varsity sports include (Men Div. III) baseball, basketball, cross country, hockey, lacrosse, soccer, swimming, tennis, track, wrestling.

Approximately 50% of students live in residences. There are 9 fraternities and 2 sororities on campus. Tuition and fees are in the $13,000 range.

SPORT	CONTACT	TELEPHONE
Hockey	Eric Hoffberg	(716) 475-5615
Lacrosse	Guy van Arsdale	(716) 475-2131

RENSSELAER POLYTECHNIC INSTITUTE

- Troy, New York
- Admissions (518) 276-6216
  Financial Aid (518) 276-6813
- 4,600 enrollment
- Very selective, 48% applicants accepted
  65% receive financial aid
- SAT scores: 577 verbal, 672 mathematics

Located 2 1/2 hours north of New York City, Rensselaer Polytechnic Institute sits on 260 acres overlooking the city of Troy.

It is known for engineering. This school also offers courses in humanities and social sciences, architecture, science and management.

Varsity sports include (Men Div. III) baseball, basketball, cross country, football, golf, hockey (I), lacrosse, soccer, swimming, tennis, track, wrestling.

There are 26 fraternities and 4 sororities on campus. Tuition and fees are in the $15,000 range.

SPORT	CONTACT	TELEPHONE
Hockey	Buddy Powers	(518) 276-8534

SETON HALL UNIVERSITY

- South Orange, New Jersey
- Admissions (201) 761-9332
  Financial Aid (201) 761-9350
- 9,400 enrollment
- 70% of students receive financial aid
- SAT scores: 459 verbal, 511 mathematics
- 67% of applicants are accepted

Seton Hall is a Roman Catholic based school founded in 1856. Tuition and fees are in the $9,000 range. The campus has 56 acres in a suburban area 14 miles from New York City. There are a large number of student commuters.

SPORT	CONTACT	TELEPHONE
Basketball	Peter Carlesmo	(201) 761-9070

SYRACUSE UNIVERSITY

- Syracuse, New York
- Admissions (315) 443-3611
  Financial Aid (315) 443-1513
- 22,100 enrollment
- SAT scores: 555 verbal, 585 mathematics
- 65% receive financial aid

Syracuse is a large independent school with 12 colleges. It is located on a 200 acre campus. A full range of Division I sports are available. Alcohol is allowed on campus. Most students live on campus. Tuition and fees are in the $12,000 range.

SPORT	CONTACT	TELEPHONE
Basketball	Jim Boeheim	(315) 443-2082
Football	Paul Pasqualoni	(315) 443-4817
Lacrosse	Roy Simmons, Jr.	(315) 443-4620

UNIVERSITY OF SOUTHERN CALIFORNIA

- Los Angeles, California
- Admissions (213) 743-5122
  Financial Aid (213) 743-6770
- 24,500 enrollment
- SAT scores: 482 verbal, 565 mathematics
- 60% receive financial aid

USC is a 165 acre, urban school with an increasing trend towards attracting better students. Admission is selective with about 73% of all applicants accepted. There is a very high interest in varsity sports. The campus has an active intellectual calendar with many visiting artists. Only 19% live in dormitories. Tuition and fees are in the $14,000 range.

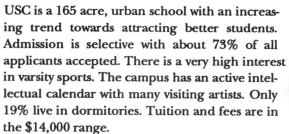

SPORT	CONTACT	TELEPHONE
Baseball	Mike Gillespie	(310)740-8444
Football	Larry Smith	(310) 740-4204
Golf	Randy Lein	(310) 740-6828
Swimming	Peter Daland	(310) 740-8444
Tennis	Dick Leach	(310) 740 6828
Volleyball	Jim McLaughlin	(310) 743-2754

STANFORD UNIVERSITY

- Stanford, California
- Admissions (415) 723-2091
  Financial Aid (415) 723-3058
- 13,300 enrollment
- 16% of applicants accepted
- SAT scores: 600+ verbal, 600+ mathematics
- 62% receive financial aid

Stanford is top notch schooling at its best. The graduate faculty is among the finest in North America. Tuition and fees are in the $16,000 range. About 87% of students live on campus. The weather is supreme and professors are excellent at Stanford.

SPORT	CONTACT	TELEPHONE
Baseball	Mark Marquess	(415) 723-4528
Cross Country	Brooks Johnson	(415) 723-1051
Football	Dennis Green	(415) 723-4511
Swimming	Skip Kenney	(415) 923-4416
Tennis	Dick Gould	(415) 723-1160
Track	Brooks Johnson	(415) 723-1051

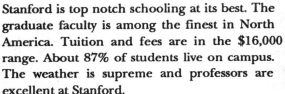

UNIVERSITY OF SOUTH DAKOTA

- Vermillia, South Dakota
- Admissions (605) 677-5434
  Financial Aid (605) 677-5446
- 6,000 enrollment
- ACTscores: 20.5 composite,
  21.2 mathematics
- 91% of students applying are accepted

The University of South Dakota is a state supported school in a town of 10,000. About 80% of all students receive financial aid. About 60% of the students live off campus. Tuition and fees are in the $25,000 range and $4,500 for out-of-state students.

SPORT	CONTACT	TELEPHONE
Basketball	Dave Boots	(605) 677-5920
Football	John Fritsch	(605) 677-5953

UNIVERSITY OF TENNESSEE

- Knoxville, Tennessee
- Admissions (615) 974-2184
  Financial aid (615) 974-3131
- 25,000 enrollment
- SAT scores: 473 verbal, 538 mathematics
- 70% receive financial aid

The University of Tennessee is a huge grouping of 19 schools and colleges. It is located in a city of 182,000 people. About 55% of all incoming students eventually graduate. Only 15% of all incoming students can come from out-of-state.

Only 30% of all students live on campus. Sports are big. Alcohol is not permitted on campus. Tuition and fees are about $1,800 in-state and $5,000 for out-of-state students.

SPORT	CONTACT	TELEPHONE
Cross Country	Doug Brown	(615) 974-1225
Football	Johnny Majors	(615) 974-1232
Swimming	John Trembley	(615) 974-1258
Track	Doug Brown	(615) 974-1225

UNIVERSITY OF TEXAS

- Austin, Texas
- Admissions (512) 471-1711
  Financial Aid (512)471-4001
- 50,000 enrollment
- SAT scores: 500 verbal, 606 mathematics
- 45% of students receive financial aid

The University of Texas is a highly selective
school and one of the U.S.'s largest. About 67%
of all applicants are accepted. About 10% of
the students live in campus housing. Tuition is
ap-proximately $1,500 in-state and $5,000 for
out-of-state students.

SPORT	CONTACT	TELEPHONE
Baseball	Cliff Gustafson	(512) 471-5732
Cross Country	Stan Huntsman	(512) 471 3931
Football	Dave McWilliams	(512) 471-4030
Golf	Jimmy Claron	(512) 471-6169
Swimming	Eddie Reese	(512) 471-7141
Track	Stan Huntsman	(512) 471-3931

UNITED STATES MILITARY ACADEMY (ARMY)

- West Point, New York
- 5,000 enrollment
- All students must meet tough entry
  requirements and have very high grades
- Admission is by nomination by members
  of congress
- U.S. citizens only

All students receive full four year scholarships as well as a salary of about $7,000 for books, uniforms and extras. West Point is an old school with a tough, no nonsense learning environment. Army has done remarkably well in varsity sports especially football for a school of its size.

SPORT	CONTACT	TELEPHONE
Football	Bob Sutton	(914) 938-3000
Hockey	Rob Riley	(914) 938-3711

UNION COLLEGE

- Schenectady, New York
- Admissions (518) 370-6112
  Financial Aid (518) 370-6123
- 2,400 enrollment
- Very selective, 51% of applicants are accepted
- 42% receive financial aid

Located on 100 acres in Schenectady (pop. 80,000), Union College is part of Union University.

Varsity sports include (Div.III) baseball, basketball, cross country, football, golf (Div. I), hockey, lacrosse, soccer, swimming, tennis, track.

SPORT	CONTACT	TELEPHONE
Football	Al Bagnoli	(518) 370-6152
Hockey	Bruce Delventhal	(518) 370-6570

WAKE FOREST UNIVERSITY

- Winston-Salem, North Carolina
- Admissions (919) 761-5211
  Financial Aid (919) 761-5181
- 3,400 enrollment
- SAT scores: 544 verbal, 620 mathematics
- 25% receive financial aid

Wake Forest is a small liberal arts school with a Baptist background. Admission is very selective with only 36% of the applicants accepted. About 80% of all freshmen graduate. Alcohol is permitted on campus. Tuition and fees are in the $10,000 range.

SPORT	CONTACT	TELEPHONE
Cross Country	John Goodridge	(919) 759-5630
Golf	Jesse Haddock	(919) 759-5619

WITTENBERG UNIVERSITY

- Springfield, Ohio
- Admissions (800) 543-5977
- 2,000 enrollment
- SAT scores: 511 verbal, 557 mathematics
- 52% receive financial aid

Wittenberg is a small church-related college. It is a selective school with 73% of all applicants being admitted. It is located on a 71 Acre campus about a 45 minute drive west of Columbus. Almost all faculty hold PhD's or equivalent. Division III sports are numerous and interest in varsity sports is high. Most students live on campus. Tuition and fees are about $13,000.

SPORT	CONTACT	TELEPHONE
Basketball	Dan Hipsher	(513) 327-6454
Football	Doug Neibuhr	(513) 327-6447
Golf	Dave Maurer	(513) 327-6453

WILLIAMS COLLEGE

- Williamstown, Massachusetts
- Admissions (413) 597-2211
  Financial Aid (413) 597-2161
- 1,900 enrollment
- Very selective, 25% of applicants accepted
- 36% receive financial aid
- SAT scores: 645 verbal, 671 mathematics

One of the most prestigious colleges, Williams is located on 450 acres in a small town of 8,500 people. Admission is very selective.

Students appear to be under a great deal of academic stress, but courses are said to be excellent.

Varsity sports include (Men. Div. III) baseball, basketball, crew (II), cross country, football, golf, hockey, lacrosse, rugby, skiing (I), soccer, squash (I), swimming, tennis, track, volleyball, water polo, and wrestling. Tuition and fees are in the $17,000 range.

SPORT	CONTACT	TELEPHONE
Basketball	Harry Sheehy	(413) 597-2201
Hockey	William Kangas	(413) 597-2036
Swimming	Carl Samuelson	(413) 597-2404

UNIVERSITY OF WISCONSIN-RIVER FALLS

- River Falls, Wisconsin
- Admissions (715) 425-3500
  Financial Aid (715) 425-3141
- 4,900 enrollment
- ACT score: 19.3 composite
- 50% receive financial aid

This school is a state assisted University located in a town of 8,000 people. It is about a 30 minute drive from St. Paul. About 78% of all applicants are accepted. Almost 60% of all freshmen graduate. It is a commuter school where three quarters of the students live off campus. Tuition and fees run about $2,000 in-state and $6,000 for out-of-state students.

SPORT	CONTACT	TELEPHONE
Hockey	Dean Talafous	(715) 425-3252

UNIVERSITY OF WISCONSIN

- Madison, Wisconsin
- Admissions (608) 262-3961
  Financial Aid (608) 262-3060
- 44,220 total enrollment
- 82% accepted, 53% enrolled
- 35% receive financial aid
- SAT scores: 500 verbal, 570 mathematics

The University of Wisconsin is a very large school located on over 900 acres. It contains 124 academic departments, 13 schools and colleges and an enormous library. The professors at UW include several Nobel prize winners, and national academy of science members. Most introductory classes contain as many as 500 students making it hard to see a professor on a one-to-one basis.

The environment outside is harsh and academic vigors are quite strong. As with all large schools, long lines and red tape are a part of every day campus life. The better programs include agriculture, engineering, business, biology, and languages.

Six out of seven students are from Wisconsin. Financial assistance is readily available. On-campus housing is a problem. Fraternities are strong making up one quarter of the student body. This Big Ten School has a national championship hockey team drawing large crowds for each game.

SPORT	CONTACT	TELEPHONE
Cross Country	Martin Smith	(608) 262-5729
Hockey	Jeff Sauer	(608) 262-3932

YALE UNIVERSITY

- New Haven, Connecticut
- Admissions (203) 432-1900
  Financial Aid (203) 432-4100
- Very selective, 18% of applicants accepted
- 60% receive financial aid
- SAT scores: 670 verbal, 690 mathematics

One of the country's best private universities, Yale is located a little over an hour northeast of New York City. Admission is highly selective and applicants must apply by December 31 to be considered. Yale attracts many top students from around the country making academic pressure highly intense.

Varsity sports (Men) include baseball, basketball, crew, cross country, fencing, football, golf, hockey, lacrosse, soccer, squash, swimming, tennis, track, wrestling. Varsity sports hold a high degree of interest for Yale students, the most popular being football, hockey and basketball.

Tuition and fees are in the $16,000 range.

SPORT	CONTACT	TELEPHONE
Hockey	Tim Taylor	(203) 432-1478

Summary

Academics is the road to success. Just ask anyone who has achieved his or her goals in the business world. The greater one's knowledge and ability to learn, the greater are one's chances to succeed. I believe that by combining academics with athletics, a truly fantastic learning atmosphere is created. Every young athlete should have a degree to fall back on. If an athletic career does not materialize, and in most cases it does not, a degree in your back pocket keeps all of your options open.

Selecting the right college or university should be done thoroughly and with much examination. Each athlete should be realistic about his/her caliber and academic training, and match them accordingly to the proper college.

When a scholarship is presented to you it can be in several ways. Some colleges will outright offer a 4-year academic payment plan which covers tuition, room and board, and books. Others will offer partial scholarships along with work-study campus jobs and low interest loans. It is important to know exactly what you are in for and to get any proposals from the financial aid office or athletic department in writing.

In recent years we have seen a tremendous growth in the popularity of college sports, both in the United States and in Canada. It does not take much insight to realize that college is the best option. Each season more and more players are drafted to the major leagues from the U.S. college ranks. The pro scouts I interviewed stated that college players bring with them a greater maturity level which is well suited for the professional world.

All in all, the college educated athlete has a much better preparation for the real world outside of sports. This is largely due to the greater emphasis on academics at the college level. College sports will set the framework for a successful future.

In recent years, the NCAA and most academic institutions have begun to vastly improve the necessary entrance requirements athletes must meet to receive athletic scholarships. This has begun the trend towards forcing students/ athletes to adequately prepare them for their collegiate programs. The ultimate goal is to produce better student performance in the classroom and increase the percentage of graduation rates. Many colleges now proudly boast of the major trend towards greater graduating percentages from their students athletes.

Life After College

ONCE A COLLEGE career is finished, life in the real world begins. When the last exam is written and the degree granted a student must be ready to begin his career plans. More and more U.S. college grads, in recent years, are catching the eyes of NBA, NFL, AL and NHL scouts. Each year more college players have the extra option of attending a pro camp.

In the majority of cases, however, graduates must enter the work force after graduation. By combining athletics with a college degree, the individual has kept all of his options open. Many employers are eagerly willing to hire an individual who has successfully combined academics and the tough competitive athletics. The competitive edge that this individual has when he graduates is exactly what many corporations or law schools are looking for.

Appendix: Teams and Roster Size Chart – Men's Sports

1990-92 Participation Study, prepared by the NCAA

Division I

Sport	Teams	Athletics	Average Squad
Baseball	271	9065	33.45
Basketball	295	4508	15.28
Cross Country	285	4067	14.27
Fencing	28	600	21.42
Football I-A	106	12737	120.16
I-AA	87	8604	98.90
Golf	266	503	1.89
Gymnastics	38	586	15.42
Ice Hockey	48	1437	29.94
Lacrosse	51	1969	38.60
Rifle	28	441	15.75
Skiing	13	244	18.78
Soccer	192	5121	26.67
Swimming	159	3929	24.71
Tennis	273	3085	11.30
Track, Indoor	225	8287	36.83
Track, Outdoor	241	8881	36.85
Volleyball	24	450	18.74
Water Polo	32	759	23.73
Wrestling	111	3343	30.12
Subtotal	2773	78615	
Crew	24	813	33.86
Squash	3	102	34.00
Total	2800	79529	

Division II
NCAA Team and Roster Sizes

Sport	Teams	Athletes	Average Squad
Baseball	156	3257	20.88
Basketball	204	3080	15.10
Cross Country	162	1978	12.21
Fencing			
Football I-A	120	10872	90.60
I-AA			
Golf	126	1318	10.46
Gymnastics			
Ice Hockey	15	491	32.71
Lacrosse	20	537	26.85
Rifle	9	66	7.33
Skiing	12	183	13.55
Soccer	108	2660	24.83
Swimming	49	1000	20.40
Tennis	153	1573	10.28
Track, Indoor	86	2319	26.96
Track, Outdoor	121	3395	28.06
Volleyball	10	120	12.00
Water Polo	7	141	20.17
Wrestling	49	1317	26.87
Subtotal	1407	34286	
Crew	6	66	
Squash	0	0	
Total	1413	34352	

Division III
NCAA Team and Roster Sizes

Sport	Teams	Athletes	Average Squad
Baseball	265	6832	25.78
Basketball	296	5227	17.66
Cross Country	248	3435	13.85
Fencing	20	329	16.44
Football I-A	221	17450	78.96
I-AA			
Golf	211	2294	10.87
Gymnastics	4	58	14.50
Ice Hockey	60	1757	29.29
Lacrosse	86	2540	29.53
Rifle	13	125	9.60
Skiing	20	306	15.30
Soccer	267	6766	25.34
Swimming	157	2834	18.05
Tennis	266	3035	11.41
Track, Indoor	145	3977	27.43
Track, outdoor	204	5824	28.55
Volleyball	24	372	15.50
Water Polo	15	251	16.73
Wrestling	120	2432	20.27
Subtotal	2642	65844	
Crew 13	485	37.33	
Squash 20	293	14.67	
Total	2675	66622	

NCAA, All Divisions
Overall Team and Roster Sizes

Sport	Teams	Athletes	Average Squad
Baseball	692	19154	27.68
Basketball	795	12815	16.12
Cross Country	695	9480	13.64
Fencing	49	929	18.95
Football I-A	534	49663	93.00
I-AA			
Golf	603	4114	6.82
Gymnastics	43	644	14.98
Ice Hockey	123	3685	29.96
Lacrosse	157	5045	32.13
Rifle	50	632	12.64
Skiing	45	713	15.84
Soccer	567	14546	25.66
Swimming	365	7762	21.27
Tennis	692	7693	11.12
Track, Indoor	456	14583	31.98
Track, Outdoor	566	18100	31.98
Volleyball	58	942	16.24
Water Polo	54	1152	21.32
Wrestling	280	7092	25.33
Subtotal	6824	178744	
Crew	43	1364	
Squash	23	395	
Total	6890	180504	

Appendix:
Teams and Roster Size Chart – Women's Sports
1990-91 Participation Study, NCAA

Division I

Sport	Teams	Athletes	Average Squad
Basketball	284	3803	13.39
Crosscountry	280	3259	11.64
Fencing	25	227	9.08
Field Hockey	76	1719	22.62
Golf	104	955	9.18
Gymnastics	67	878	13.10
Lacrosse	33	820	24.84
Skiing	11	149	13.58
Soccer	82	1858	22.66
Softball	174	2949	16.95
Swimming	163	3627	22.25
Tennis	279	2704	9.69
Track, Indoor	221	5545	25.09
Track, outdoor	239	5863	24.53
Volleyball	270	3405	12.61
Crew	7	204	29.14
Totals	2315	37963	

Women's - Division II
NCAA Team and Roster Sizes

Sport	Teams	Athletes	Average Squad
Basketball	206	2758	13.39
Cross Country	154	1579	10.25
Fencing	3	18	6.00
Field Hockey	13	256	19.67
Golf	18	152	8.47
Gymnastics	19	244	12.83
Lacrosse	12	323	26.90
Skiing	11	91	8.27
Soccer	51	1060	20.78
Softball	161	2657	16.50
Swimming	54	1061	19.65
Tennis	154	1418	9.21
Track, Indoor	86	1713	19.92
Track, Outdoor	117	2504	21.40
Volleyball	193	2397	12.42
Subtotal	1252	18230	
Crew	2	24	12.00
Totals	1254	18254	

Division III
NCAA Team and Roster Sizes

Sport	Teams	Athletes	Average Squad
Basketball	296	3990	13.48
Cross Country	232	2640	11.38
Fencing	20	206	10.31
Field Hockey	128	2739	21.40
Golf	23	167	7.25
Gymnastics	17	227	13.33
Lacrosse	73	2189	29.99
Skiing	19	206	10.86
Soccer	185	3863	20.88
Softball	245	4118	16.81
Swimming	179	3159	17.65
Tennis	278	3019	10.86
Track, Indoor	140	2734	19.53
Track, Outdoor	197	3824	19.41
Volleyball	278	3911	14.07
Subtotal	2310	36994	
Crew	3	77	
Totals	2313	37071	

NCAA, All Divisions
Women's Overall Team and Roster Sizes

Sport	Teams	Athletes	Average Squad
Basketball	786	10551	13.42
Cross Country	666	7478	11.23
Fencing	48	451	9.40
Field Hockey	217	4714	21.72
Golf	145	1274	8.79
Gymnastics	103	1348	13.09
Lacrosse	118	3332	28.24
Skiing	41	446	10.89
Soccer	318	6781	21.32
Softball	580	9724	16.77
Swimming	396	7847	19.82
Tennis	711	7141	10.04
Track, Indoor	447	9992	22.35
Track, Outdoor	553	12190	22.04
Volleyball	741	9713	13.11
Subtotal	5870	92983	
Crew	12	305	25.45
Totals	5882	93289	

Notes:
1 Participation totals are adjusted to reflect all institutions sponsoring each sport.
2 Sports sponsored by fewer than 10 institutions are not included in this survey.
3 Totals in several sports include mixed (men's and women's) teams.

Source: The National Collegiate Athletic Association, January 15, 1992

Appendix: The Scholastic Aptitude Test (SAT)

As high schools may vary widely as to their grading standards. The Scholastic Aptitude Test (SAT) was developed to better and more fairly indicate how a student may do academically in college. A combination of high school grades and test scores are thus used by college admissions officers to consider each applicant in making admissions decisions.

The SAT is a multiple choice test from both verbal and mathematical areas. The verbal questions are designed to test your vocabulary, verbal reasoning and understanding of what you read. The math section tests your ability to solve arithmetic problems, elementary algebra, and geometry.

In addition to the SAT, each test booklet also includes a test of Standard Written English (TSWE). It is also a multiple choice test with the purpose of placing each student into the English course matched to his/her ability.

The test includes:
- 2 SAT - verbal sections
- 2 SAT - math sections
- 1 TSWE section
- 1 section of equating questions (verbal, math, or TSWE). This section is not included in your final score. It is used to try out questions for future SAT's.

On the following few pages are sample questions similar to those you may find on the SAT. In a test situation you will be given 30 minutes to complete each section.

Section 1 - Verbal

Each question below consists of a word in capital letter, followed by five lettered words or phrases. Choose the word or phrase that is most nearly opposite in meaning to the word in capital letters. Since some of the questions require you to distinguish fine shades of meaning, consider all the choices before deciding which is best.

Example:

good   a) sour   b) bad
     c) red   d) hot
     e) ugly

The answer is b)

1. cherish   a) despise   b) utilize
     c) aspire   d) encourage
     e) compete

2. veto   a) predict   b) discuss
     c) approve   d) display
     e) evaluate

3. extinguish   a) graze   b) revive
     c) correct   d) intrude
     e) exceed

4. ceremonious   a) active   b) enjoyable
     c) permanent   d) informal
     e) widespread

5. symmetry   a) exclusion   b) imbalance
     c) isolation   d) immensity
     e) validity

6. document   a) edit   b)withhold
     c) reproduce in full
     d) write for pay   e) leave unsupported

7. harbor
   a) enlighten
   b) burden
   c) permit
   d) prepare for
   e) turn away

8. breadth
   a) rarity
   b) mobility
   c) complexity
   d) narrowness
   e) roughness

9. noxious
   a) diffuse
   b) unique
   c) beneficial
   d) latent
   e) static

10. reprehensible
   a) matchless
   b) praiseworthy
   c) interesting
   d) difficult to control
   e) seldom recognized

11. scanty
   a) adept
   b) copious
   c) prosaic
   d) candid
   e) mellow

12. adulation
   a) initiation
   b) vilification
   c) injustice
   d) purification
   e) deliverance

13. prodigious
   a) questionable
   b) approximate
   c) ultimate
   d) adjacent
   e) minuscule

14. tensile
   a) inelastic
   b) genuine
   c) tough
   d) sympathetic
   e) inharmonious

15. amity
   a) strife
   b) irrelevance
   c) realism
   d) topicality
   e) unseemliness

Each sentence below has one or two blanks, each blank indicating that something has been omitted. Beneath the sentence are five lettered words or sets of words. Choose the word or set of words that, when inserted in the sentence, best fits the meaning of the sentence as a whole.

Example:

Although its publicity has been _____, the film itself is intelligent, well-acted, handsomely produced, and altogether _____.

    a) tasteless...respectable
    b) extensive...moderate
    c) sophisticated...amateur
    d) risque...crude
    e) perfect...spectacular

The answer is a)

16. The ambassador's papers are not _____ reading, but one who reads slowly and attentively will be richly repaid.

    a) petty   b) valuable   c) insightful
    d) easy   e) plausible

17. It is inaccurate to describe Hopkins as a crusader for progressive reforms, for, although he debunks certain popular myths, he is not really _____ of change.

    a) an advocate   b) a censor   c) an adversary
    d) a caricature   e) a descendant

18. He was lonely and might have considered himself miserable were it not for a kind of hysterical _____, which he could neither account for nor _____.

    a) depression ... enhance
    b) apathy ... tolerate
    c) contentment ... enjoy
    d) merriment ... conquer
    e) sorrow ... comprehend

19. Occasionally _____ strain of bacteria appears, changed by some molecular misprint from what was once only _____ into a life-taking poison.
    a) a new ... an epidemic
    b) apathy ... tolerate
    c) contentment ... enjoy
    d) merriment ... conquer
    e) sorrow ... comprehend

20. The discussions were often _____, degenerating at times into name-calling contests.
    a) lofty   b) auspicious   c) acrimonious
    d) lethargic   e) pragmatic

Select the word or set of words that best completes each of the following sentences.

21. Many sportswriters have been caught up in the activities about which they write and have become advocates and _____ when they ought to have been _____.
    a) promoters...colleagues
    b) participants...collaborators
    c) apologists...critics
    d) opponents...antagonists
    e) disputants...defenders

22. His inability to fathom the latest trends in art led him to fear that his critical faculties had _____ during his long absence.
    a) diversified   b) atrophied   c) converted
    d) predominated   e) multiplied

23. Though her lecture contained ideas that were provocative and systematically presented, her style of delivery was so _____ that I actually dozed off.

a) galling   b) pungent   c) desultory

d) soporific   e) theatrical

24. Fuentes' subtly persuasive arguments for continuity in Latino culture _____ readers to recognize that the future cannot be _____ from the way they treat their past.

Each question below consists of a related pair of words or phrases, followed by five lettered pairs of words or phrases. Select the lettered pair that best expresses a relationship similar to that expressed in the original pair.

Example:

yawn:boredom

a) dream...sleep

b) anger...madness

c) smile...amusement

d) face...expression

e) impatience...rebellion

The answer is c)

25. **judge:courthouse**

a) physician...hospital

b) clergyman...library

c) farmer...house

d) visitor...hotel

e) mathematician...computer

26. **mumble:indistinct**

a) relent...gentle

b) stumble...graceful

c) enunciate...clear

d) define...difficult

e) grunt...shrill

27. **colors:spectrum**
    a) experiments...laboratory
    b) panes...glass
    c) guests...party
    d) letters...alphabet
    e) leaves...tree

28. **tadpole:frog**
    a) stream...river
    b) acorn...oak
    c) politician...diplomat
    d) negative...photograph
    e) student...graduate

Section II - Mathematical

1. If x-7 = 5-x, then x =
   a) -6   b) -1   c) 1   d) 6   e) 12

2. A gymnast competed in a meet and received the following scores for three events: 9.5 for bars, 8.7 for balance beam, and 8.8 for floor routine.. What is the average (arithmetic mean) of these three scores?
   a) 8.9   b) 9.0   c) 9.1   d) 9.2   e) 9.3

3. On a number line, if point P has coordinate -3 and point Q has coordinate 5, what is the length of segment PQ?
   a) 2   b) 4   c) 5   d) 8   e) 64

4. If (20 + 5) + (30 + N) = 70, then N =
   a) 30   b) 40   c) 50   d) 60   e) 70

5. If $(x + 3)^2 = (x - 3)^2$, then x =
   a) 0   b) 1   c) 3   d) 6   e) 9

6. Ms. Jones borrowed $1,000 for a year. The cost of the loan was 6 percent of the amount borrowed, to be paid back together with the loan at the end of the year. What was the total amount needed to pay off the loan?
   a) $1,000.60
   b) $1,006.00
   c) $1,060.00
   d) $1,600.00
   e) $6,000.00

7. If $\frac{5}{x} = 1$ and $\frac{y}{2} = 3$, then $\frac{(3+x)}{(y+3)} =$

   a) $\frac{5}{6}$ b) $\frac{8}{9}$ c) 1   d) $\frac{9}{8}$ e) $\frac{6}{5}$

8. Which of the following is the greater of two numbers whose product is 220 and whose sum is 10 more than the difference between the two?
   a) 5   b) 10   c) 22   d) 44   e) 55

9. _____._____ 1
                 P

   If two points, Q and R, are each placed to the right of point P on line 1 above so that 2PQ = 3PR, what will be the value of RQ?
   a) 1   b) 2   c) 2   d) 3
   e) It cannot be determined from the 2 5 3 2 information given

10. | X | Y |
    |---|---|
    | 1 | 4 |
    | 2 | 5 |
    | 3 | 6 |

    If x is a number from column X and y is a number from column Y in the table above, how many different values are possible for x + y?
    a) nine   b) eight   c) seven   d) six   e) five

The above questions are examples of a typical SAT exam. Most students prepare for several weeks prior to writing their SAT. Many students buy books preparing them to score well on the tests. There are also specialty instruction courses, like those taught by Stanley Kaplan, which are intended only to increase one's score on the test. You can obtain the instruction books at any book store and you can sign up for the SAT prep course at any college or university.

Answers To Sample Test

Section 1 - Verbal

1. A		15. A
2. C		16. D
3. B		17. D
4. D		18. D
5. B		19. D
6. E		20. A
7. E		21. C
8. D		22. B
9. C		23. D
10. B		24. C
11. B		25. A
12. B		26. C
13. E		27. D
14. A		28. B

Section II - Math

1. D		6. C
2. B		7. B
3. D		8. D
4. A		9. A
5. A		10. E

Selected Bibliography

1. Cass, James and Birnbaum, Comparative Guide To American Colleges, New York: Harper and Brown, 1989.

2. Fiske, Edward B. Selective Guide to Colleges, Toronto: Random House of Canada, Limited, 1985.

3. Hockey East Yearbook, Orono, Maine, 1989.

4. NCAA Guide for the College-Bound Student Athlete, edited by Michael V. Earle, Misson, Kansas. April 1988.

5. Taking The Sat, Princeton, New Jersey, Educational Testing Service, 1987.

6. The NCAA News, Lexington, Kentucky, Dec 5, 1988.

7. NCAA, 1990-91 National Collegiate Championships Manual, Overland Park, Kansas. September, 1991.

8. Interview, Greg Summers, Asst. Director of Publishing, NCAA. February, 1992.

9. Interview, Rick Campbell, NCAA Statistics. Kansas, U.S.A. February, 1992.

10. Peterson's Guide to Four-Year Colleges, 1991. Peterson's Guides, Princeton, New Jersey, Susan W. Dilts, Editor

11. The Gourman Report. A Rating Of Undergraduate Programs in American and International Studies. Seventh Edition, Dr. Jack Gourman, 1989, National Education Standards.

12. National Directory of College Athletics, 1991-92, Collegiate Directories Inc. Cleveland, Ohio.

1992-93 Financial Aid Application
Deadlines and Instructions

Harvard-Radcliffe Financial Aid Office
8 Garden Street, 312 Byerly Hall
Cambridge, MA 02138

(617) 495-1581

Deadlines:

By February 14, 1992 the Financial Aid Form (FAF) must be submitted to the College Scholarship Service by all U.S. citizens and permanent residents.

By April 1, 1992 you must submit to the Financial Aid Office (FAO):

- The Harvard-Radcliffe student Financial Aid Application and Reference Form.

  - Your Parents' 1991 federal income tax form(s), signed and complete with all schedules and W2 Forms.

  - Your 1991 federal income tax form, signed and complete with your W-2 Form and, if filed, any schedules.

  - Any additional forms that are required, such as the Divorced/Separated Parent's Statement, the Business/Farm Supplement, the Financial Statement for Students from Foreign Countries, or the Supplement for New Applicants.

  - Any additional statements that your custodial parent(s) need to submit, such as a child support statement, a Social Security benefits statement, or a notarized statement of tax non-filing status.

In addition, U.S. citizens and permanent residents must submit an accurate Student Aid Report (SAR) as soon as they receive it. The SAR will be mailed by the College Scholarship Service to your permanent address as listed on the FAF.

Please remember to:

- Write your name and **social security number** on all materials submitted.

- Be sure that all tax forms submitted are **signed federal forms** and include **all schedules and W2 Forms.**

- Please note that the Student Activity Sheet (pg. 5 of the student Financial Aid Application) is **required** each year.

It is your responsibility to read and follow the enclosed instructions. It is also your responsibility to ensure that your application is complete. Please be sure to check that we have all the required application materials before leaving for the summer. You and your parents are always welcome to contact your Financial Aid Officer with questions or concerns.

Financial Aid Officers by Class

Class of 1995   Sally Champagne
Class of 1994   Caroline Quillian Stubbs
Class of 1993   Aurelio Ramirez

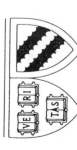

HARVARD·RADCLIFFE

Instructions

Financial aid applicants for 1992-93 are responsible for reading and following all instructions below which pertain to them. We recommend that you send all materials to our office together in the enclosed addressed envelope.

Must my parents wait until they have completed their 1991 federal income tax return before filling out the Financial Aid Form?

While it is not necessary to delay submission of the FAF until the parents' federal income tax return for 1991 is completed, the FAF should represent the actual 1991 income as accurately as possible. This is especially true if families want to avoid making changes later. For example, the Student Aid Report (SAR) for the Pell Grant Program is generated from the FAF and will reflect the information reported on the FAF. If the FAF contains estimated income data, the SAR will need to be changed later to reflect actual income data. Whether actual or estimated figures are used, it is important that the FAF be filed with the College Scholarship Service by **February 15, 1992.**

What if my parents are separated or divorced?

Ordinarily each parent should submit financial information. We have mailed the FAF to your home address. The **custodial** parent's FAF should be completed and sent to the College Scholarship Service for processing. **You must contact the Financial Aid Office to obtain a Divorced/Separated Parent's Statement for your non-custodial parent.** The **non-custodial** parent's Divorced/Separated Parent's Statement should be sent directly to the FAO. If either parent has remarried, his or her application form should include information about the new family unit, including the current spouse's income and assets and information concerning the dependents in that household.

What if my parents will be filing their 1991 federal income tax return after April 1st?

Your parents should attempt to complete the tax return by April 1st even if they do not send the form to the IRS until April 15th. If your parents have filed for an extension with the IRS, they must submit a copy of that extension form to the FAO. Your application will not be acted upon until the completed copy of your parents' federal income tax return is received.

What if my parents will not file a 1991 tax return?

If your parent(s) do not file a federal income tax return, they must submit a notarized statement stating they do not file and listing all sources and amounts of income by April 1, 1992. Please use the following statement on a separate piece of paper for notarization.

"I (we) have not filed and will not file a 1991 U.S. Income Tax Return. All sources and amounts of income for 1991 are listed below. All information on the Financial Aid Form/Student Aid Report which will be used to calculate my child's federal aid eligibility is complete and correct."

Source   Amount of income

_____   _____

_____   _____

_____   _____

_____   _____

_____
Signature

_____
Notary

_____
Seal

What if my parents operate a business or a farm?

Please file the FAF Business/Farm Supplement along with the FAF. These supplements are available in the Financial Aid Office upon request. If a 1991 corporate or partnership return was filed, you must submit it to the FAO.

What if my brother or sister will also be a student at Harvard/Radcliffe?

Each sibling must submit a complete set of financial aid applications including an FAF, tax forms, and a Harvard/Radcliffe student Financial Aid Application.

What if my brother or sister is a student at another college in 1992-93?

We need to know the educational plans of each of your siblings in college or graduate school and the cost of each to your parents. If you do not know this information when you complete the FAF, please inform us in writing as soon as you do know.

Do I need to submit a tax form for 1991?

Yes, if you filed one for 1991. If you filed a tax form but did not keep a copy of it, please contact your local IRS office to obtain an official copy. If you did not file a tax form for 1991, check the appropriate box on the student Financial Aid Application.

What if my family has unusual circumstances which are not fully explained by the FAF or student Financial Aid Application?

If you need to provide additional details or explain unusual situations enclose a written explanation with your student Financial Aid Application. In addition, please feel free to contact the Financial Aid Office about any concerns you have.

What if I am an international student?

Canadians should use the Canadian student instruction sheet when filling out their financial aid applications. Other international students should file a student Financial Aid Application as well as the Financial Statement for Students from Foreign Countries. All necessary forms are available in the Financial Aid Office. Parents' tax returns are required of all students of all nationalities. We do not normally mail award letters to international students but hold them for students to pick up in the fall. If you would like your award letter mailed, please inform us in writing.

How do I send the Information on the FAF to other agencies or Institutions?

We have pre-stamped your FAF so that the information will be sent to Harvard and the Pell Grant Program. To apply for state scholarships or to other institutions, you must write their names and code numbers in the space provided on the FAF and enclose the proper fee.

Do I need to apply for a state scholarship?

Yes, if you are a resident of Connecticut, Maine, Maryland, Massachusetts, Pennsylvania, Rhode Island, Vermont or Washington, D.C. If you are a previous state grant recipient, you are responsible for following through on your state's own renewal procedures and filing your application on time. If you are a resident of a state listed above, but are not a current recipient of a state scholarship, you are also encouraged to apply. Please contact the Financial Aid Office for details. **Students who are eligible for state funds but do not apply or apply too late will not receive additional Harvard-Radcliffe funds to cover the lost state aid.** Specific renewal procedures for the various states are as follows:

Maine, Massachusetts, Rhode Island, New Hampshire—A special state Financial Aid Form (FAF) should be enclosed. If not, contact us immediately.

Connecticut, Pennsylvania, Vermont—Application and instructions from state if student is current recipient. Student should contact state program if materials are not received by February 1, 1992.

Maryland, Washington, D.C.—State scholarship office supplies applications and should be contacted for renewal information.

How do I apply for a Pell Grant?

You apply for a Pell Grant by submitting a completed FAF to the College Scholarship Service. Using the FAF to apply for a Pell Grant does not involve any additional cost to you and insures that you will be considered for eligibility for the Pell Grant Program. **All applicants who are citizens or permanent residents of the US are required to file for a Pell Grant before they will be considered for assistance from other programs. Your FAF will generate a Student Aid Report (SAR), which will be mailed directly to you by the College Scholarship Service. Your Harvard/Radcliffe financial aid application will not be considered complete until we receive an accurate, signed SAR.**

What is the College Work-Study Program?

The College Work-Study Program (CWSP) is a federally funded program designed to help financially needy students meet educational expenses through term-time and summer work either on campus or in other non-profit agencies. The advantage of work-study eligibility is that the federal government pays 70% of your wages and your employer only 30%. Because CWSP funding is limited, eligibility is restricted to students with the most need. For more information about jobs, please contact the Student Employment Office.

What If I only want to apply for a Stafford Loan through an outside source?

According to federal regulations, **all students** applying for a Stafford Loan must fill out the FAF. You should complete the FAF in the spring, mail it to the College Scholarship Service, and keep a copy to attach to your loan application. In the summer you should obtain a loan application from your local or previous lender, and should mail it and the copy of the FAF to the Financial Aid Office. If you are only applying for a loan, please write "Loan Only" on the FAF you send us.

What is the purpose of the reference form and whom should I ask to complete it?

The reference form will be used to help us fund student awards from sources with particular restrictions, and where appropriate, to help us provide needed reports to our donors. We write to our financial aid donors to keep them informed of the progress of the students who are recipients of their funds and to encourage donors to contribute further. The information provided on the reference form will **have no effect on the amount of aid you will receive**. Please give the reference form to someone **within the University** who knows you academically. **All students must submit a completed reference form.**

When will I find out about my financial aid award?

Notifications for applicants who have filed on time are usually mailed in July. Late applications will be considered as they are completed. If an application is completed late, we cannot guarantee an award decision by Fall Registration.

What if my permanent address changes?

Any changes should be submitted to the Student Data Office, located on the 5th floor of Holyoke Center, and directly to the Financial Aid Office. Address labels for mailings are computer-generated so it is important that you file an accurate address with each office.

What if I am returning from a leave of absence?

If returning from a leave, follow all of the regular instructions and deadlines in filing your 1992-93 financial aid application materials. Be certain that you are current in your loan repayment and that your Term Bill is paid in full. Please contact your Financial Aid Officer with any questions.

How will I know that my financial aid application is complete?

It is **your** responsibility to check on the application before you leave school for the summer. The Financial Aid Office does mail out reminders, but by then the application may already be late and your award severely delayed.

PLEASE KEEP A PHOTOCOPY OF THE FAF, YOUR STUDENT APPLICATION, TAX FORMS, AND ANY OTHER INFORMATION SUBMITTED TO THE FINANCIAL AID OFFICE IN CASE SOMETHING IS LOST.

HARVARD·RADCLIFFE

**Office of Admissions
and Financial Aid**
Byerly Hall, 8 Garden Street
Cambridge, Massachusetts 02138
617/495-1551

Freshman Financial Aid Application

Valid for entrance in September 1992 only
Submit by February 15, 1992

Name of Applicant
(please print or type)

Last/Family	First	Middle	Jr., etc.

Home Address

Number and Street	City	State/Country	Zip/Postal Code

U.S. Social Security Number (if any) ☐☐☐ - ☐☐ - ☐☐☐☐

This is the application for all financial aid funds administered by the Committee on Admissions and Financial Aid. The forms required and deadlines are the same for Early Action and Regular Action applicants. For all the documents listed below, use the best figures available to you, and estimate if necessary to meet deadlines. Complete copies of 1991 federal income tax returns will be required before financial aid is credited to your account and awards may be revised if figures differ substantially, so it is important to estimate carefully. An application for aid will not jeopardize your chances for admission; however, late applications for aid cannot be assured of full consideration. If you receive any outside scholarships usable at Harvard and Radcliffe or if your financial situation changes and you no longer wish to be considered for financial aid, please notify us in writing.

☐ **Financial Aid Form (FAF):** Complete the FAF (or SAAC in California) and mail it to the College Scholarship Service (CSS) with the appropriate fee as soon after January 1st as possible, but no later than February 15, 1992, in order to assure a financial aid decision by mid-April. (If your parents are separated or divorced, use information from the parent with whom you live.) Send us a photocopy if the FAF is completed after February 15th. Keep a copy for your own reference in case the FAF is lost in the mail or misfiled. Students who are not U.S. citizens or permanent residents and whose parents live in a foreign country (except Canada) should contact our office for the "Financial Statement for Students from Foreign Countries" which is more suited to the kinds of financial information available to foreign families.

Institutional Aid Application: This Harvard-Radcliffe Freshman Financial Aid Application requests information not included on other forms and should be completed by all financial aid applicants.

Federal Income Tax Returns: Send us signed photocopies of all pages and schedules of your own and your parents' 1991 federal income tax returns, including photocopies of the W-2 forms, with your Freshman Financial Aid Application. If the 1991 returns have not been completed, send 1990 returns.

Divorced/Separated Parent's Statement and Tax Returns: If your parents are divorced or separated, your non-custodial parent should submit a Divorced/Separated Parent's Statement (available upon request from the Financial Aid Office), with signed photocopies of all pages and schedules of the most recent federal income tax return.

Business/Farm Supplements and Tax Returns: If either of your parents is self-employed or owns a business or farm, he/she should submit a Business/Farm Supplement (available upon request from the Financial Aid Office) for each business or farm in which any interest is held. If there are corporations or partnerships, attach copies of the most recent business tax returns (Forms 1065, 1120, 1120S, K-1).

Estate or Trust Tax Return: If the student, the parents, or other children are beneficiaries of an estate or trust, submit the appropriate schedule K-1 of Form 1041 or Form 4970.

Your aid application will not be considered until all requested documents and information have been received. Be sure to notify us if you have an unavoidable delay. We want to be able to offer you aid if it is needed. Please help us to help you by following instructions and meeting deadlines.

First

Last

(please print or type)
Name of Applicant

If any family members have attended Harvard and Radcliffe, give names, class years and relationship to you: _____

_____

Are you a resident of CT, DC, ME, MD, MA, NH, PA, RI or VT? ☐ Yes ☐ No If yes, you must apply for your state scholarship. Forms should be available from your high school guidance counselor or you may be able to apply by using the Financial Aid Form.

Make and year of family automobiles _____

Are you a citizen of the United States? ☐ Yes ☐ No

If no, what is your country of citizenship? _____

your visa status _____ your alien registration number? _____

Our Estimate of Costs for the 1992-93 Academic Year:
(based on 1991-92 figures, and will increase somewhat for 1992-93)

Tuition and Fees	$16,560
Room and Board	5,520
Personal Expenses	1,620
Travel (2 round trips;	0 - 1,600
depending on your home state)	
Total Estimated Costs	$23,700 - $25,300

Your Estimate of Resources for the 1992-93 Academic Year:

(Use this area to think about how much aid you will need for college and what sources of funding you and your family have access to. We realize that your figures below are only estimates.)

From your parents' income and assets.................................... 1. $ _____

From loans taken out by your parents................................... 2. $ _____

From a non-custodial divorced/separated parent....................... 3. $ _____

From friends and relatives.. 4. $ _____

From your summer 1992 earnings....................................... 5. $ _____

What are your total savings and assets? $ _____
Enter one-third of total here... 6. $ _____

From state scholarships or other outside awards which you have already been granted........... 7. $ _____

Name of organization giving grant: _____

From Social Security, Veteran's or other student benefits............... 8. $ _____

From other sources (describe: _____)........ 9. $ _____

Your estimated total resources (add 1-9).............................. $ _____

Amount of aid requested (subtract total estimated resources from total estimated costs)............ $ _____

Feel free to attach a letter of explanation if your family has special circumstances or unusual expenses, or if you feel there are any other details which will help us to understand more completely your financial situation.

Name _____ _____ _____ Social Security Number _____ — _____ — _____
      Last/Family   First   Middle   (if held)

Home Address _____ _____ Telephone _____ — _____ — _____
             Street and Number   Apartment

_____ _____ _____ Date of Birth _____ / _____ / _____
City   State/Country   Zip/Postal Code   Month   Day   Year

Answer the questions that apply to you or your family, and go on to the Statement of Understanding.

Student Information

1. Give details of any **student** assets: total amount   source (e.g. parents' savings, gifts from relatives, earnings, etc.)

     cash and savings $ _____   _____

     Uniform Gifts to Minors $ _____   _____

     stocks, bonds, CD's and $ _____   _____
     other investments

     Other **student** assets (car, real estate, etc.)

asset	purchase price	date of purchase	current value	amount owed
_____	$ _____	_____	$ _____	$ _____
_____				

2. Complete for trusts in **student's** name (and send photocopy of most recent Form 1041 or 4970):

     established by _____ when? _____

     type of trust _____ total value $ _____ annual income? $ _____

     terms of distribution _____

Parent Information

3. Are parents separated or divorced? ☐ Yes ☐ No

If yes, a College Scholarship Service Divorced/Separated Parent's Statement and the most recent tax form must be submitted by your non-custodial parent. You may request the form from the Financial Aid Office, and photocopy it if you are applying to several schools.

Date of separation _____ Date of divorce _____

Has either parent remarried? Mother? _____ When? _____ Father? _____ When? _____

Please list your non-custodial parent's name, address, occupation and employer. If address is not available, attach an explanation.

Name _____ Occupation _____

Address _____ Employer _____

4. Is either parent self-employed or does any family member hold an interest in any business or farm? ☐ Yes ☐ No

If yes, a College Scholarship Service Business/Farm Supplement is required. You may request the form from the Financial Aid Office, and photocopy it if you are applying to several schools. Please also send us a copy of the most recent corporate or partnership return if the business is other than a sole proprietorship.

Name of business or farm: _____ Parent's position: _____ _____ % owned _____

5. List all those in your household dependent upon (i.e., supported by) your parent(s) in 1992-93. Include yourself, your parent(s) (or your custodial parent and stepparent if your parents are divorced), your brothers and sisters, and other relatives. Attach a separate sheet if necessary.

		Educational Information, 1991-92				Educational Information, 1992-93			
Full Name	Age	Name of school or college	Year in school or college	Total scholarships and grants	Amount paid by parents	Name of school or college	Full-time? Yes No	Live at school/ college Yes No	Parents claim as tax exemption in 1992? Yes No

6. Complete for custodial parent(s):

Check: ☐ father ☐ stepfather ☐ guardian ☐ other

Name _____

Occupation/Employer _____

Title/Position _____

Years with current employer _____

Check: ☐ mother ☐ stepmother ☐ guardian ☐ other

Name _____

Occupation/Employer _____

Title/Position _____

Years with current employer _____

7. Indicate parents' income from any of these sources:

	1991	1992
Housing and other living allowances for military, clergy, educators, etc	$ _____	$ _____
Workers' Compensation or other untaxed disability benefits	$ _____	$ _____

Indicate voluntary income reductions:

	1991	1992
Contribution to tax-deferred annuity (SRA, 401K, 403B)	$ _____	$ _____
Withheld for reimbursement accounts		
for dependent care	$ _____	$ _____
for medical costs	$ _____	$ _____

8. Are there assets other than trusts held in names of other brothers or sisters of the student applicant?

type	total value	child's name
_____	$ _____	_____
_____	_____	_____

9. Is any family member (other than student applicant) beneficiary of a trust? Send photocopy of most recent Form 1041 (or 5227) for each trust.

established by _____ for _____ when _____

type of trust _____ total value $ _____ annual income $ _____

terms of distribution _____

10. Are any partnerships listed on Schedule E of parents' most recent tax return? ☐ Yes ☐ No

If yes, complete the following:

name of partnership _____ year entered partnership _____ total amount invested

$ _____

11. Other real estate (other than primary home, business or farm): _____

	Date of purchase _____	Purchase price _____	Current value _____	Current debt _____

12. Parental Debt:

	Current amount owed	Payments in 1992
First mortgage	$ _____	$ _____
Second mortgage or home equity loan	$ _____	$ _____
Auto loan(s)	$ _____	$ _____
Educational	$ _____	$ _____
Other _____	$ _____	$ _____

13. Child support and alimony paid and/or received:

	Received in 1991	Paid in 1991
Child support for all children	$ _____	$ _____
Child support for student applicant	$ _____	$ _____
Alimony	$ _____	$ _____

14. Indicate resources that will be available for parents' retirement:
Check all that apply and list present accumulated value of IRA's, Keogh's, TDA's, and insurance in space provided.

☐ Social Security	☐ Ira/Keogh Plans .... $ _____
☐ Civil Service	☐ Tax-deferred Plans .... $ _____
☐ Military Pension	☐ Single Premium Insurance .... $ _____
☐ Union Pension	☐ Other (Specify) .... $ _____
☐ Employer Pension	☐ State Pension .... $ _____

Statement of Understanding

I/we understand that information provided on this and other documents may be shared with the applicant, with other agencies from which we are requesting aid, and with donors if aid is offered and accepted.

I certify that I have not defaulted on any federally supported student loan (Stafford, Perkins, SLS or PLUS) and that I do not owe a refund on any federally supported student grant (Pell, SEOG, or SSIG) at any institution.

I/we certify that all information presented here is correct at this time, and that we will send timely notice of any significant change in family income or assets, financial situation, college plans of other children or of the receipt of other scholarships or grants.

Signature of parent or guardian _____ Date _____

Signature of student applicant _____

ABOUT THE AUTHOR

David Lahey grew up in Nepean, Ontario, East of Toronto. His is a graduate of Hamilton College in Clinton, New York, where he was the recipient of an athletic scholarship for hockey. He is a businessman based in Kingston, Ontario, and lives there with his wife and three children.